THE ART OF LIVING
CHINESE PROVERBS AND WISDOM

This book is edited and designed by the Editorial Committee of *Cultural China* series.

Text by Hong Yingming
Annotation by Wu Yansheng and Ding Liangyan
Translation by Tony Blishen
Design by Wang Wei
Photos by Getty Images and Quanjing

Copy Editor: Diane Davies
Editors: Wu Yuezhou, Cao Yue
Editorial Director: Zhang Yicong

Senior Consultants: Sun Yong, Wu Ying, Yang Xinci
Managing Director and Publisher: Wang Youbu

ISBN: 978-1-60220-163-7

Address any comments about *The Art of Living: Chinese Proverbs and Wisdom* to:

Better Link Press
99 Park Ave
New York, NY 10016
USA

or

Shanghai Press and Publishing Development Co., Ltd.
F 7 Donghu Road, Shanghai, China (200031)
Email: comments_betterlinkpress@hotmail.com

Printed in China by Shanghai Donnelley Printing Co., Ltd.

1   3   5   7   9   10   8   6   4   2

THE ART OF LIVING
CHINESE PROVERBS AND WISDOM
A Modern Reader of the *Vegetable Roots Discourse*

COMPILED BY HONG YINGMING
ANNOTATED BY WU YANSHENG AND DING LIANGYAN
TRANSLATED BY TONY BLISHEN

Better Link Press

PREFACE

The *Vegetable Roots Discourse*
—A Treasury of Eastern Wisdom

The traditional culture of China was a self-sufficient agricultural civilization of a clear inward-looking nature that developed centripetally, was perfect in itself and placed an emphasis upon holism and harmony. The traditional culture of the West was an oceanic culture of a markedly extrovert character that expanded outwards, that explored, that advanced actively and emphasized an individualistic and competitive spirit. The present era is one in which Western and Chinese cultures are tending to merge and where each civilization mirrors the other. Each civilization has its own particular content and values. Western culture concerns itself with individualism, regards human rights as important, pursues liberty and wealth and is one that Eastern cultures could well learn from. At the same time, Western culture would find it worth learning from Eastern culture and the value it places upon inner reflection in life and its striving after harmony and tranquility. Whilst both cultures may adhere to the great twentieth-century sociologist Fei Xiaotong's (1910–2005) principle of "unto each its own beauty," they must further "see the beauty of others" and "beautify the beauty in all" before they can achieve the bilateral reciprocity of "world community."

For the Westerner wishing to achieve a direct and vivid understanding of Eastern culture and a sense of Chinese culture, the *Vegetable Roots Discourse* is an excellent primer.

The *Vegetable Roots Discourse* is a remarkable Ming dynasty (1368–1644) collection of quotations, aphorisms and proverbs published during the Wanli reign (1573–1620). The compiler and author was Hong Yingming, a man immersed in the essential aesthetic of Chinese culture. His style name was Zicheng and given name Huanchu Daoren, meaning a practitioner of Daoism who sought to return to the purity of his original mind. Why was this book given the title *Vegetable Roots Discourse*? The Northern Song dynasty (960–1127) scholar Wang Xinmin (1071–1110) said that someone who could "chew on vegetable roots" could "achieve everything." The average person prefers to eat the leaves or the heart of vegetables, very few are willing to eat the root because it is coarse, tasteless and difficult to swallow. The kind of person who is willing to eat it, and does so with relish, possesses a nature of imperturbable self-cultivation. He does not pursue a life of material luxury and does not easily succumb to the temptations of material desire, while his ability to live an ordinary life with enthusiasm and enjoyment makes it possible for him to do anything he wishes.

With this concept in mind, Hong Yingming compiled his popular *Vegetable Roots Discourse*, subsequently a widely circulated treasury of Eastern culture. Through figuratively eating vegetable roots it is possible to calmly and cheerfully discuss heaven and earth, ancient and modern, and love and passion. What a fascinating prospect this is.

The *Vegetable Roots Discourse* combines the traditional Chinese cultural wisdom of the Confucian doctrine of the mean, the Daoist concept of non-action (*wuwei*) and the Buddhist doctrine of transcendentalism into a panorama of an ideal life for which the modern generation yearns and in which it is possible to lead an unencumbered and enlightened life in a natural landscape of beauty, tranquility and humanity, or within an ordinary life of coarse tea and cold rice. As the German philosopher Martin Heidegger (1889–1976) put it, quoting a line from Hölderlin (1770–1843): "poetically dwells the man" (dichterisch wohnet der Mensch).

The principal point of the *Vegetable Roots Discourse* is an emphasis upon the beauty of the harmony of traditional Chinese culture. This subdivides into three main aspects: harmony between man and nature, harmony between man and society, and harmony between man and his inner being. These may be exemplified as harmony with heaven, harmony with earth, and harmony with man.

The *Discourse* advocates harmony between man and nature—harmony with heaven. In Eastern cultures man is not the master of all things, so it is impossible to adopt an anthropocentric viewpoint of self-supremacy that controls, plunders and contaminates all nature. Instead, we should coexist harmoniously with nature so that "Heaven and Man are as One." Because heaven and man are one, the body and soul of heaven and earth are thus human, the auspicious stars and clouds of the heavens are the vital energy of human joy, and thunder, lightning, tempest and storm are the emanations of human anger. Man is of the same body and soul as heaven and earth and the latter possess great powers for the healing of humanity. Borrow the support of the natural world to regulate the spirit, wander among the rocks and springs of the hills and woods and the longing for the bustle and hubbub of the world will gradually expire, thereby transcending the mundane, discarding the secular world and combining both body and spirit in purity.

The *Discourse* also advocates harmony between man and society—harmony with earth. One should not regard other people as hell, our sense of compassion may be a heaven for others. Society is formed of innumerable individuals, you comprise me and I also comprise you, thus we should exercise mutual toleration, mutual devotion and mutual achievement and not scheme against each other, exploit each other or harm each other. Traditional Chinese culture has always valued harmony itself above all and revered the harmonious qualities of good nature, kindness, amiability and peace. If, nowadays, as we show concern for individualism and human rights, we can also show a little more tolerance and concern for others, then interpersonal relationships will become both more harmonious and more beautiful. The Eastern cultural concept of harmonious coexistence may solve the difficult problem of the "clash of civilizations." It is only through a strengthening of dialogue, mutual respect and understanding, and harmonious coexistence that Eastern and Western cultures can further strengthen and develop in accord and harmony.

Finally, the *Discourse* advocates harmony between

man and his inner being—harmony with man. There is no greed, anger or stupidity to man's inner being, no contradictions or suffering, it is a state of harmony. When we have no greed in our heart, we cannot take the road of no return towards the pursuit of desire. Without anger's root in our hearts we are filled with gratitude towards others and towards all things of the universe. When there is no stupidity in our hearts, our life is a little calmer and clearheaded, a little more relaxed and unperturbed. A heart filled with the spirit of enthusiastic advance is obviously all very praiseworthy, but when fine ideals receive a bloody nose at the hand of reality we always need to see through to the question of attachment and heal the wounds of sorrow. In this, the *Vegetable Roots Discourse* is a miraculously effective cure.

Historically, the *Vegetable Roots Discourse* has always had a wide circulation as an excellent primer for the study of Chinese culture and has appeared in a number of different editions. Two comparatively important editions are the Ming and Qing dynasty (1644–1911) block-printed editions. The Ming edition consists of two sections, "former" and "latter," the "former" containing 225 items and the "latter" 135, a total of 360 in all. A copy of this edition is held in the Japanese Cabinet Library, Shoheizaka Gakumon Academy in Tokyo. The Qing edition is a single volume divided into a number of chapters such as "self-cultivation," "social entertainment," "leisure" and so on. It is the Ming edition that has been used as the basis for this translation.

The *Vegetable Roots Discourse* has had a worldwide influence and there have been a number of translations. The present translation has its own particular characteristics. For the last fifty years I have nurtured a passion for the traditional culture of China and have lived the life advocated in the *Vegetable Roots Discourse*. At the same time I have tried hard to study and absorb the essence of Western culture. Consequently, the commentary in this translation is a realization of the mind of Hong Yingming, but it also takes account of the particular spiritual characteristics of Western culture. Tony Blishen, the London-based translator, is imbued with Western culture but he has also spent some time living and working in China and has a unique knowledge and experience of Chinese culture. He has previously translated two of my books into English, *Chinese Zen* and *The Power of Enlightenment: Chinese Zen Poems*, the latter has been used as teaching material in a Western university and both have been widely welcomed in universities and colleges in China. I am grateful for his dedication and am confident that this new translation of his will give readers the same kind of vigorous spiritual stimulus. At the same time, I would like to thank the editorial team for the strenuous efforts that they have made towards the world circulation of the *Vegetable Roots Discourse*.

VEGETABLE ROOTS
DISCOURSE

1. Those who uphold virtue may be lonely for a while but those in thrall to power will suffer isolation for eternity. The person of perception sees beyond the material world and takes into account the importance of reputation after life. He would rather experience the loneliness of a moment than perpetual desolation.

The society of today is obsessed with the pursuit of wealth and the glamour of social activity. However, the sages of ancient China warned that moral character was far more important than fame and fortune. Those who seek fame and profit may well take pleasure in the visitors thronging at their door but such pleasure can only be temporary. Those who seek spiritual values may not immediately succeed in all but their reputation, for nobility of moral character will spread throughout posterity. Thus, on the one hand we may enjoy activity but on the other we should be able to endure loneliness. Though we may be lonely for the moment, those who know us best will continue to know us, encounter us and speak well of us in the world of the future.

2. A shallow acquaintanceship with the ways of the world may suffer less from its corruption but a depth of worldly experience may bring a similar depth of cunning. Thus, a gentleman should be plain and simple rather than worldly-wise, and frank and open rather than meanly cautious.

Man's original nature is pure, simple and virtuous. But as we grow to maturity we are inevitably tainted by our contact with the secular world. As we learn various skills so do we acquire worldly habits. The young person entering society for the first time may, because of limited experience, still retain a purity of character and treat others frankly and sincerely. But those experienced in the ways of the world often brim with sophistication and urbanity, act with a slippery caution and manipulate people heartlessly. However, the gentleman of cultivation who has experienced the vicissitudes of life and tasted the luxury of the mundane world will still maintain the truth and virtue of his innate nature and live with generosity and an open mind.

3. The true character of a gentleman, like the sun in a blue sky, should not be concealed from others but his talents should be hidden like pearls and jade.

The Warring States period (475–221 BC) philosopher Xunzi (c.313–238 BC) said in his treatise *On Learning*: "Stone contains jade and the hills shine thereby, water contains pearls and rivers are thus beautiful." The character of the cultivated gentleman shines forth; he is openhearted and treats people with sincerity. His talents resemble the jade within a stone or the pearls in the water, gently graceful rather than opulently displayed. The flaunting of talent inevitably arouses envy and disaffection in others. Thus, magnanimity of heart should be a principle of behavior and diffidence in talent an art in conduct.

4. Pure are those who do not draw close to power and avarice but those who do draw close and yet remain uncorrupted are purer still; noble are those who know not trickery and stratagem but nobler still are those who know them yet do not employ them.

The Eastern Han dynasty (25–220) historian Ban Gu (32–92) said in the *Book of Han*: "The ancients saw shame in dealing in power and profit." That is to say that attaching oneself to the rich and powerful with the aim of acquiring wealth and fame was something that the cultivated gentleman regarded as shameful. Those who voluntarily distance themselves from the red dust of the inducements of the mundane world and are aware of cunning and deceit but do not employ them are even more worthy of respect. This is because their self-control and ability to resist the attractions of wealth and fame are superior to those of others.

5. That the ear should hear what it would rather not hear and the mind think what it would rather not think, that is the whetstone upon which the practice of virtue is honed. To hear nothing that is not pleasing and to think of nothing that does not bring joy to the heart is to drown oneself in poison.

Laozi (dates unknown), the thinker and philosopher of the Spring and Autumn period (770–476 BC) said in the *Daodejing*: "Fine words are not honest and honest words are not fine." Though the sound of criticism may fall hard on the ear and discomfort the mind, it can urge us towards genuine virtue so that we recognize our shortcomings in time to correct them and avoid taking the crooked path. "The keen edge of a sword blade derives from the whetstone and the fragrance of plum blossom grows from bitter cold." If everything in life was merely honeyed words and matters always turned out to suit us, it would be no different to a trap disguised with a carpet of flowers, sapping our will—truly "there is life in suffering but death in pleasure."

6. An ill wind and torrential rain drives birds and fowls to distress; a clear sky and warm wind gladdens grass and trees. Thus it is that in heaven and earth a day may not pass without kindness, nor the heart of man lack a day without joy.

One of the highest reaches of ancient Chinese philosophy is the belief that heaven and man are as one. All the sentient beings of the universe and the men and affairs of society are interrelated in a state of mutual influence that constitutes one great common structure of life. Man is part of nature and thus must be influenced by nature. When the weather is bad, beasts and birds are frightened and fearful and the heart of man easily afflicted by sorrow. In clement weather, trees and grass burgeon and the heart of man rejoices. The *Daodejing* emphasizes, "The Way is of and in the Natural World." Nature is not only the embodiment of the Way, the supreme principle of man and society; it is also mankind's best teacher and source of law. In nature, when the wind howls and the rain pours, all creation's creatures suffer in desolation and decay but when nature's wind is gentle and the sun is warm, the vitality of creation reasserts itself. Thus, we can see that heaven and earth in peace and harmony can raise life; that a mood of joy can nurture character. We should live in the world with optimism and pass each day in happiness and joy.

7. Strong and delicate, sweet and spicy are not true flavors, true flavor is insipid; the complete man is neither miraculous nor extraordinary, he is ordinary.

Laozi said in the *Daodejing*: "True music is without sound, ultimate form lacks shape and morality remains hidden and unsung." The Warring States period philosopher and thinker Zhuangzi (c. 369–286 BC) wrote: "The complete man is without self, spirits are without achievement and sages are without fame." The uttermost achievement of self-cultivation is to "reach the extreme of glory and return to the ordinary." Those who reach a high degree of self-cultivation have already surpassed and overcome the need to manifest their own merits and realize that, to the contrary, it is the humdrum and ordinary that matter and that within the ordinary there is a great and enduring strength.

8. Heaven and earth exist silent and immoveable yet the pulse of life never ceases; the sun and moon rush headlong through night and day yet their light has shone unchanged for an eternity. Hence the gentleman must think actively and constructively in his leisure but maintain the flavor of leisure in his activity.

The *Book of Changes*, the well-known classic of Chinese philosophy, says: "One dark one light, one male one female, *yin* and *yang*, that is the Way." Consequently, there is nothing in heaven and on earth that is not governed by *yin* and *yang* and there is no change that is not governed by the four seasons. Heaven and earth and the universe were born of a combination of *yin* and *yang*. In the four seasons, movement and stillness follow each other in endless change. The gentleman of wisdom and intelligence may achieve a profound understanding of the principles of change in human affairs from the laws of the motion of heaven and earth, thereby achieving a grasp of the principle of the appropriate relationship between movement and stillness. Thus in affairs one may prepare by taking precautions ahead of time and by judging the need for tension or relaxation. One should not over-relax one's vigilance when at leisure but prepare for lightning from a clear sky and guard against the unforeseen. When occupied and busy one should adopt an air of calmness and face events without confusion and in a composed frame of mind.

9. Seated alone in self-contemplation deep in the calm of night, one starts to feel the emergence of a state of Nirvana and the retreat of illusion. At this point one may experience a sense of existing in a microcosm that is utterly without distraction; thereafter it becomes difficult to feel both reality and yet rid oneself of illusion, and one experiences a great sense of shame and of the need to mend one's ways.

The sages of Confucianism, Buddhism and Daoism all paid particular attention to the practice of self-reflection and emphasized the examination and awareness of one's heart and mind. When one escapes the clamor of the mundane world of dust and sits alone in meditation, it is possible to achieve a clarity of mind that is pure one moment and turbid the next, that is calm one moment but entangled by desire the next. This unceasing interchange between the sincerity of the true mind and a state of illusion is the greatest enemy of meditation and self-examination. Self-examination requires one to be sufficiently aware of one's base desires, to overcome their interference with the true mind, and to anchor one's mind in a state of tranquility and freedom. Buddhism teaches us that one may be a Buddha in one thought and a demon in the next.

10. Benevolence may breed harm, thus in joy one should always look back. Defeat may perchance bring success, thus one should never abandon hope.

The philosopher Confucius (551–479 BC) of the Spring and Autumn period, who founded the Confucian school of thought, advocated the doctrine of the Middle Way in which "too far" was reckoned to be as bad as "not enough." To overdo things may lead one in precisely the opposite direction to the one intended and thus turn good to bad. When you are at the height of power and achievement, it is difficult to reach a perfect conclusion; when you have been showered with generosity and favor, then disaster may follow on its heels. Thus, when filled with self-satisfaction, one should be clearheaded and not exhaust one's advantages for the sake of wealth and office. Equally, one should not so easily give up in despair the moment one encounters a setback. Keep going; success is round the corner.

11. Those who live on pigweed and spinach are for the most part men of jade-like purity. Those who dress in silk and satin and dine on delicacies are for the most part servile flatterers. Hence, hardship fosters strength of spirit while luxury saps moral character.

Someone who is at peace with himself can sleep well under a roof of straw and find the taste of vegetable roots delicious—this is known as "eat vegetable roots and everything is achievable." Those who can exist on a diet of plain tea and simple food and calmly face a life of honest poverty are naturally of upright character. Those who hanker after fine clothes and rich food are easily driven by desire and will bow and scrape for a trifle. To be content with one's lot calms the mind and to be free of desires elevates the character.

12. In life one should broaden the field of one's heart so that none should have grounds for grievance; after death one's bounty should flow so that none should be deficient in remembrance.

To deal with people as one should, one needs a heart of tolerance and thought for others in everything. One should not be mean minded and haggle over every ounce. Though there may be a limit to physical life, the life of the spirit has a long-lasting influence. In this limited physical life one should perform good deeds and accumulate a store of bounty. In this way, even though the body dies and decays, the spirit lives on in the remembrance, thoughts, and praise of others.

13. Where the road is narrow, leave space for others; when food is tasty, share it with others. This is the best way of achieving peace and happiness in the world.

Man is the sum of his social connections. The multitude of connections that binds each person to the other constructs the space in which each of us exists and lives. The best way of living a life that is stable in both body and mind is to not always have self at the forefront of one's mind but to think of others at all times and places. The giving of roses leaves one with scented hands. To help others is an achievement for self as well. The ability to share with others enables us to experience the very peaks of happiness and joy in harmony with others.

14. It takes no great effort to conduct oneself properly, merely rid oneself of passion and thus acquire virtuous status; erudition requires no especial addition of knowledge, reduce one's attachment to material acquisition and one may become a sage.

In society today, individual worth is judged by the quality of external activity, a person's scholarship and erudition is determined by purely academic achievement. The ancients, however, considered that whether in conduct or learning, the key lay in purity of emotion, an indifference to the crowd and a will that was not disturbed by the wealth and fame of the secular world. This is the profound cultivation that earns the respect of others. Otherwise, an attachment to worldly indulgence and a mind turbid with impurity will be no more than the contemptible stink of lust and carnality, despite wealth and position and a cartload of erudition.

15. *Be chivalrous in making friends, and simple and straightforward in conduct.*

In the grossly materialistic society of today, where people scheme against each other for personal gain, mutual feeling is both false and empty. When a major crisis occurs, everyone goes their own way or even turns to enmity. The *Dream of the Red Chamber*, one of China's four great novels, describes how one of the characters, Wang Xifeng, "was too clever by half in hatching schemes, harmed others and paid with her own life." Thus, one should conduct oneself with honesty and with a little less cunning and rather more straightforwardness.

16. Do not be forward in seeking gain or backward in advancing virtue or spreading good works. One should not seek to enjoy more than one's share or settle for standards of conduct lower than one ought.

The Western Han dynasty (206 BC–AD 25) historian Sima Qian (c. 145 or c.135 BC–?) wrote in the *Records of the Grand Historian of China*, the first Chinese biographical history: "When the empire is prosperous all come for gain, when the empire is in chaos all leave for gain." In this life it is easy to become obsessed with material enjoyment, gaining favor and advancing one's own interests, so we fight to get to the front and fear to fall behind, tossing virtuous conduct and good works aside. The *Book of Changes* says: "As with the vigor of heaven so should man strive, as with the bounty of earth so should man grow in virtue." The gentleman should add to his virtue by increasing his moral cultivation, expanding his activities and making a contribution. He should study the ways of heaven with strength and resolution, work energetically for the good of all, expand his achievements and learn how the earth has substance but is yet acquiescent and harbors all sentient beings.

17. In conduct it is better to give way, for stepping back is but a prelude to stepping forward; to treat people generously is to gain good fortune and to bestow advantage on others is to lay the foundations of one's own advantage.

In work and in life the habitual and constant struggle with others not only leads to a loss of dignity but also to difficulties in the achievement of one's objectives, and both sides suffer. The peasant planting rice steps backwards as he plants. It is only by stepping backwards that he can ensure that the rice sprouts are planted in straight lines. Modest withdrawal is not a matter of negative compromise but is rather an act of intelligent wisdom. In China, there has long been the saying: "The gentleman treats others generously" believing that in so doing, the bestowal of kindness also enriches the giver and is a propitious act. The cultivated man moves in an air of friendship and reaps the reward of acts that profit both others and himself.

18. Arrogance of achievement gains not a word of praise; repentance of sin brings not a word of condemnation.

An ancient Chinese proverb says: "Self-satisfaction provokes harm, modesty brings benefit." Arrogant self-satisfaction very quickly provokes resentment and brings painful consequences in its train. Contrariwise, even in the case of deep sin, genuinely sincere repentance and renewal will bring forgiveness so that life may once more shine in glorious of virtue.

19. A virtuous reputation and high principles should not be enjoyed in isolation, they should be shared with others to avoid harm and to protect the self; shameful conduct and a sordid reputation should not be completely repudiated, taking some responsibility upon oneself may sheath the sword of self-glorification and foster virtue.

An excessive reputation for honor and glory is not necessarily a good thing. In his *Treatise upon Destiny*, the writer Li Kang (c. 196–c. 265) of the State of Wei (220–265) during the period of the Three Kingdoms (220–280) wrote: "The tallest tree of the forest must of necessity suffer the wind's destruction." Criticism is the companion of the finest reputation. Hence there is no harm in sharing the benefits of fame with others. Conversely, when one is wronged and reviled, one should not entirely place the blame on others but should reflect and take the initiative in accepting some of the responsibility so that one may whet the blade of one's morality and integrity.

20. Leave space in everything and even the Creator himself will not be jealous and demons and spirits will not harm you. If every undertaking must be achieved to the utmost then those who carry things to the extreme will suffer interference from without even if they escape inner turmoil.

The sages of ancient China advocated the Middle Way, believing that in affairs one should hold to the middle ground, there should be a sense of what is appropriate and there should be balance. Extreme methods in the conduct of affairs are, like an over-tautened violin string, easily snapped and matters taken to an extreme can only reverse their course. Hence, one who conducts himself properly will always allow others room for the exercise of ability and good sense and space in which to reap benefit. If one attempted to secure all advantage to oneself and sought a selfish perfection in everything, even if one could bear the internal mental burden, it would almost certainly invite external trouble.

21. A true Buddha exists in every family and a true path exists in daily life. If one can act with sincerity and kindness, adopt a kindly expression and speak with tact, and live as one with parents and brothers in mutual understanding, then that is a thousand times better than meditation and exercises in inner tranquility!

The Confucians were proponents of "rectification of the heart, cultivation of self, management of family, governance of the state and pacification of all under heaven." They believed that if a person consciously adjusted body and mind and, within the family, respected the old and loved the young and enabled father and mother, brothers and wives and children to co-exist in mutual harmony, then such a person had the ability to manage affairs of state, rule the people and become an enlightened sovereign loved and revered by his subjects. Consequently, in Confucian eyes the family was the best situation in which to temper one's personality. Living as a family in sincerity with a kindly expression and tactful speech combined with gentility of attitude, eliminates discord and suspicion between parents and brothers, achieving harmonious unity and happiness that is the ideal state of life and living.

22. A love of activity is like lightning in a cloud or a flickering flame; a love of solitude resembles the ashes of a dead tree. A principled mind and body requires still clouds where birds may soar and calm waters where fish may leap.

The cultivation of mind and body requires an environment where movement and calm are balanced to suit the comprehension of the Way. A restless temperament and agitated mind disturbs one's nature and makes it difficult to achieve tranquility. Conversely, a mindset immersed in the utter extinction of all experience is like a pool of dead water where life has lost its vitality and living becomes totally dull. The best state is one of calm, of clouds and still water, a simplicity of mind where the birds can soar and fish leap. Calm, yet without loss of agility of mind, stable yet brimming with vitality.

23. Be not too severe in the attacking of faults, consider how much may be borne; in the instruction of virtue do not aim too high, consider how much may be achieved.

In the education of others, whether in praise or criticism, one should have a sense of proportion and avoid excess. If there is fault, a whiff of condemnation or severe criticism may not only defeat the purpose of instruction but also arouse a counter psychology that negates the very essence of education. In the inculcation of virtue, the targets should not be set too high or the demands made too severe, one should consider what measure of achievement is possible. The Confucians believed in "severity to oneself but leniency to others," the treatment of others requires a suitable degree of tolerance. This is both a form of self-cultivation and a kind of wisdom in outward behavior.

24. The dung beetle makes filth yet becomes the cicada that sups upon the dew of the autumn wind; rotten straw is without light but produces the glowworms that shine so brilliantly in summer. Knowledge is to understand that purity often springs from filth and that light is born of darkness.

The ancients discovered from their life experience that the larva of the noble cicada that ate the wind and drank dew lived in the filth of a dung heap. The glowworm that shines on a summer evening is also born out of the filth of rotten straw. One can see from this that purity and filth are not absolute opposites but may, under certain conditions, be mutually interchangeable. So is the life of man. An evil environment has always been the whetstone upon which character and great causes are honed, and lotus flowers emerge unstained from the mud. In times of dirt and darkness one should maintain the confidence to transform filth into light, so that one may greet a glorious future.

25. Pride and arrogance are born of empty affectation; once rid of this behavior the spirit of righteousness will shine forth. Sensuality and lust are a vain illusion; once they are eradicated upright honesty will appear.

A classic Buddhist text, the *Platform Sutra*, states: "The nature of all living things was originally pure." Buddhism believes that the nature of man, like heaven and earth, the sun and moon, was originally both pure and undefiled and glorious. Greed, hatred and ignorance are like the dust that obscures a mirror and that also darkens the mirror of the soul. Consequently, one should "constantly sweep and clean to prevent the accumulation of dust." Only by frequently cleansing the soul of dust and ridding it of vexation and delusion can the mirror of one's inner being shine forth in glory and purity.

26. Once sated with food one cannot recall the difference between rich and plain; once sated with sex one cannot recall the stirrings of lust. Hence one should use the sense of regret after the deed to counter the obsession of the moment and fix one's nature so that no act lacks principle.

Mengzi (c. 372–289 BC), the thinker and leader of the Confucian school of thought at the time of the Warring States said: "Appetite and lust are matters of basic nature." A starving man is filled with a fierce longing for food; the stirrings of lust prompt a desire for female beauty but once these longings and desires are sated they lose their interest. In life man is filled with certain curiosities, longings and impulses. Once they have been experienced one discovers that they are nothing much. People who have had their fill of the red dust of the mundane world and who once more encounter something enticing are able to maintain equilibrium of heart and are not easily misled by appearances.

27. The official at court must not lack a sense of the hills and forests; dwelling amongst hills and streams one must remember the stratagems of court.

A man who occupies a high position, scheming in the cockpit of fame and profit, is easily entangled in complicated affairs and suffers thereby. At this point he must maintain a simplicity of outlook before he can retain an attitude of unruffled calm. With time on one's hands and in the comfort of home, away from the cares of office, it is easy to turn lazy and slothful. Here, one must retain a sense of social responsibility and maintain an interest in current affairs. In such a life, whether involved in affairs or not, one may advance or retreat at will in proper order.

28. In conduct do not strive after merit, to be without fault is merit enough; in one's dealings with others do not expect gratitude or recompense, not to suffer complaint is recompense enough.

In daily life when people help others they frequently do so out of a sense of arrogant self-satisfaction, hoping that others will show gratitude and quickly reciprocate. This is a demonstration of extreme selfishness and of no benefit at all in raising one's state of virtue. Cultivated people require a spirit of selfless dedication and should not always be in pursuit of some utilitarian recompense that shows them in a good light. In helping others, one should not strive for gratitude and recompense for the help. It is enough that there is no fault and that you have not aroused the hatred of others. That is the greatest achievement.

29. To labor in the performance of good works is the height of virtue but to suffer thereby is of no comfort to the mind. A certain measure of indifference to success is best and to be worn out by care helps nobody.

It is praiseworthy to possess professional ambition and a sense of responsibility and to work hard. Nevertheless, to know only work and profession and to work so hard as to be both physically and mentally exhausted will have a counter-effect and lead to a loss of interest in life itself. A man who is indifferent to fame and profit may well be considered to be of good character. Nevertheless, an excess of the lofty-minded avoidance of desire may lead to a cold detachment in which there is no feeling of responsibility towards either state or society. This kind of detachment has neither value nor significance. In everything, too much is as bad as not enough, good may turn to evil and the original gale of virtue become just a scented hint on the wind.

30. One who labors but sees no road ahead should consider his first intentions; one who has achieved success should consider what is to come.

The man building a venture is full of satisfaction and self-confidence. However, once a setback is encountered, it is easy to become dispirited and downcast and to give in to despair. There is another phenomenon—"The hundred *li* traveler falls at the ninetieth," in which many people on the point of success lose their grip and fail at the last moment so that all that has been achieved already is lost for lack of a final effort. In such a situation what is most needed is to retain one's confidence and courage. Think of your first intentions and motivation and you can dispel the predicament that confronts you more easily and not give up so lightly.

At the point of recognition and success it is exceptionally easy to become complacent and to have no regard for the way forward. In this case, a failure to value one's good fortune, an indulgence in licentious behavior and blind greed may mark the place where glory is actually the beginning of downfall, so that the peace and stability of one's final years becomes a sea of mud.

31. Though the wealthy should be generously openhearted, conversely, they are often mean and suspicious. This is the behavior of the poor and lowly. How then is wealth to be enjoyed? The clever man should be discreet but many are ostentatious, this is the defect of the stupidly clever! How can this not fail?

The wealthy should by rights be openhearted and generous in their treatment of people before they can adopt grand airs. If one enjoys wealth and rank but one's treatment of others is harsh and lacking in benevolence, that is to arouse universal condemnation. How could such wealth be long maintained? Highly talented people are much the same. They stand out in a crowd but the merest hint of self-display and boasting will cause people to shun them. It is only a modest bearing that will win the respect of others and establish one in an impregnable position.

*32. Dwell humbly to know the perils of ascent, live
in darkness to know the dangers of light; keep still to
know the fatigue of activity, nurture silence to know
the agitation of verbosity.*

There is a proverb that says: "The participant is puzzled;
the onlooker is clear." Situated at a height there is, of
course, the grandeur of looking down upon the world but
there is also the misery of "the unbearable cold of high
places," the loneliness at the top. It is just that it is difficult
to detect the danger you are in as you climb upwards.
By contrast, those below can clearly see the towering
mountain mass above them. It is only in tranquility that
you can comprehend the weariness of hectic scheming;
only in silence that you can, from a contrasting standpoint,
better grasp the agitation of ceaseless chatter. Changed
circumstances bring a different view. If we can observe life
from a different point of view, we can become more awake
and aware.

33. Jettison the attractions of wealth and achievement and you may escape the mundane world; abandon the attractions of virtue and benevolence and only then may you enter the realm of light.

Wealth, and glory, reputation and fame are the obsessions of the worldly. Ascetic practice is a means of tempering oneself to avoid the harm of a longing for wealth and fame. Originally there was no great harm in the enjoyment of wealth and fame. However, if one's inner being becomes fixated upon them, one becomes their slave. What is the point of then speaking of freedom and detachment?

34. Fame and desire may not harm the heart absolutely, prejudice and illusion are the weevils that gnaw at the mind; licentious behavior is not necessarily an obstacle to the path of self-cultivation, self-assumed cleverness is the wall that stands in the way of virtue.

Compared with the hounds of desire and fame, the unhealthy characteristics of prejudice of heart, perversions of thought, self-righteousness and self-assumed cleverness are much more harmful to the character. The Seven Emotions and Six Desires (The Six Desires are generally taken to be Color, Sound, Scent, Touch and Means; the Seven Emotions are Joy, Anger, Grief, Fear, Love, Hatred and Lust) are very apparent and thus easy to correct or overcome. However, inner prejudice and self-assumed cleverness can cloud the judgment and are much more difficult to detect. In the end they can hinder the growth of a proper wisdom and render clever people stupid.

35. The mind of man is complex and the ways of the world rugged and steep. When you cannot get through you should know how to step back; when you can get through you should know the merit of giving way.

It is impossible to predict the changing moods of man, and human relationships are complicated and ever changing. The path of life has never been smooth, it is full of twists and turns and changes of direction. Thus, when we encounter a pit that we cannot cross we should understand how to step back and not rush forward. We should understand how to slacken our pace and regard withdrawal as progress, so that we can see the situation clearly and avoid wasting time and effort. Similarly, when things are going well and the wind fills our sails, then that is the time for modesty and prudence and to politely give way so as to avoid disaster caused by faulty judgment born of over-confidence.

36. In dealing with a rogue it is easy to be severe but difficult not to feel hatred; in dealing with a man of virtue it is easy to show respect but difficult to demonstrate the correct degree of politeness.

It is not difficult when dealing with an uncultivated and ill-behaved rogue to adopt an attitude of severity, what is difficult is to empty the depths of one's heart of loathing and treat him well and to help and educate him. When you discover the mistakes and faults in others, indulging in criticism and hatred rather than instructing or helping demonstrates a similar lack of moral responsibility. Most people feel respect for a deeply cultivated person of virtue and prestige, what is difficult is to treat them with true politeness. Over-politeness can descend into flattery and with that there comes an element of falsity.

37. Better to be simple in mind rather than clever and retain some righteousness to repay heaven and earth; better to decline a life of luxury and delight in plain living and leave some purity for the world.

The ancient saying goes: "Cleverness is the enemy of intelligence." Man's thought and wisdom are limited. Using a fistful of clever trickery to scheme for petty advantage may seem like getting the better of others but in the end one is damaged by one's own prejudices to the harm of others and without benefit to self. Laozi said: "The Way is of and in the Natural World." In life one should learn from all the sentient beings of the universe and indulge less in cunning trickery and more in a natural simplicity. This is the only means of retaining a nature that is both upright and honest, leaving a reputation for pure simplicity and gaining a life that is tranquil and harmonious.

38. Devilry first seizes the mind, subdue the mind and the devils depart; to rid the mind of wayward thoughts, subdue one's mood and they will no longer intrude.

The Buddhist *Garland Sutra* says: "The mind is like a painter's brush, capable of depicting everything that exists." The devils and demons of life have their source in the evil thoughts of the mind. If the mind remains immovable, then the devils and demons from outside retreat without a battle. Dealing with ruthless and tyrannical barbarity is much the same. Controlling the violent unreason of the outside world first requires control of the thoughtless frivolity of one's own heart. A mind like still water and as stable as a rock will keep out evil and defeat poison.

39. The instruction of disciples resembles the raising of daughters; one should emphasize severity in the control of their coming and going and prudence in their friendships. If they become close to someone undesirable it is tantamount to planting bad seed in a fertile field; it will be difficult to grow good rice.

There is an ancient saying: "Stand next to vermilion and you will look red, stand next to ink and you will look black." When someone is growing up and their habits are being formed and their characters molded, the demands on them should be severe and they should be strictly controlled, particularly in the matter of close friends who should be selected for their virtue. Otherwise, making friends with a pack of ne'er-do-wells will exert a bad influence and lead to the acquisition of bad habits, rather like planting bad seed in a fertile field. Once the wrong path is taken, education becomes extremely difficult.

40. When the attractions of desire appear, take no joy in their lucky convenience or fortuitous advantage, to do so is to fall into an abyss; when the path of principle appears, do not be put off by its difficulty and step back, once that step is taken you will be separated by a mountain range.

A proverb says: "Learning is like paddling a boat against the current, unless there is progress there is retreat; the heart is like riding a horse on a plain, easy to loose but difficult to rein in." Man is prone to the Seven Emotions and Six Desires and finds it difficult to avoid the temptations of the outer world. Even its slightest infection makes it easy to let oneself go and enjoy it, thus taking step after step to corruption. Ascetic practice is like paddling a boat upstream, relax but a little and one loses a thousand miles. In the face of physical desire, one should increase vigilance and understand how to suppress desire; in the pursuit of truth one should concentrate all one's efforts and not slacken them otherwise previous achievement will be thrown away and all will come to naught.

41. Those of a generous disposition who treat themselves well will also treat others well and generosity will abound; those of a stingy disposition who treat themselves stingily will treat others badly as well and meanness will be all. Thus it is that the gentleman in his habits should be neither over-generous nor too parsimonious.

Pamper oneself and you will pamper others and all will be extravagance and luxury; treat oneself harshly and you will treat others harshly and all will be mean and stingy. Extravagance and luxury may well be enjoyable but they very easily unsettle the mind and lead to over-indulgence in pleasure; stinginess may well be economical but it easily saps the energy from life and renders it without interest. Hence, a gentleman will strike an appropriate balance between generosity and parsimony, neither the noisy commotion of luxury and extravagance nor the tedium of miserliness.

42. Others possess riches, I have humanity; others have rank, I have righteousness; a true gentleman should not be constrained by the power of others. A determined man may overcome circumstances and a resolute man may master his own temperament. A gentleman does not suffer himself to be molded by the movement of fate.

Mengzi wrote: "One should not be corrupted by wealth and honor, altered by poverty or bent by power." A man of profound cultivation and a gentleman of parts will not be enticed by the external attractions of high office and a generous salary but will steadfastly maintain his inner integrity and righteousness in the face of riches and power. Mengzi also said: "A concentrated will may move the spirit and a concentrated spirit may move the will"—meaning that when will and spirit are combined one may control the inner workings of physical life. As the thought moves so the workings of the body move with it. In the same way, the internal workings of the physical body can further strengthen the concentration of the will and spirit. Zhuangzi said, "The gentleman may master the material." A gentleman of determination may control the external world through mind alone and, in a state that transcends the external material world, remain impervious to the whims of fate.

43. If you do not stand tall when improving your character it is like dragging your clothing in dust or washing your feet in mud, how then are you to transcend the commonplace? If you do not withdraw a pace when engaging with the world and act like a moth drawn to a flame or a goat caught in a fence, how are you to achieve peace and happiness?

In the cultivation of character and spirit one should aspire to lofty ambitions before one can expand the horizons of one's mind and transcend the commonplace and ordinary. Wallowing in the mire with people of mundane mind is akin to dragging clean clothing in the dust or trying to wash your feet in mud. To conduct oneself properly in engagement with the world requires an understanding of modesty and tolerance, space must be left in the conduct of affairs—this is the concept of "step back a pace to see the world's extent" advocated in Chinese philosophy. To scurry about seeking favor or petty advantage in everything will put one in a position where it is difficult either to go forward or to withdraw. Where would there remain room for happiness and joy in life?

44. Learning requires one to gather one's wits and concentrate the mind. If, in the cultivation of virtue, one remains wedded to fame and achievement in affairs, there can be no true attainment; to study but to interest oneself only in mere recitation will never achieve profundity of mind.

The acquisition of learning requires an effort of will and wholehearted concentration as well as the exclusion of external interference and distraction. Otherwise, to study with a mind filled with a strong sense of fame and profit is comparable to the way in which a man who considers himself to possess integrity but who, nevertheless, thinks of nothing but prestige and reputation, can never achieve true cultivation or progress. Failure to study in depth and merely seeking an elegance of literary style will neither achieve anything substantial nor gain anything of real value.

45. Each and every one possesses a charitable heart and even a butcher stands but a little distance from the pure, unsullied Weimojie (an early Buddhist hermit believed to have been born in India and to have achieved some wealth in early life); each and every place possesses its own interest and a straw hut and a palace of gold are not far apart. It is just that when caught up by lust and desire the very shortest distance becomes a vast gap.

The Buddhist *Garland Sutra* says: "Strange, all sentient beings are innately wise and virtuous but once in the grip of delusion they can no longer attain this wisdom and virtue." The reason for the differences that exist between ordinary people and sages, sentient beings and Buddhas, is because within the heart of man there is avarice, hatred and obsession. Sweep away these delusions and it is possible to nurture a charitable heart and a true interest. Only arouse charity of heart and even a butcher or headsman can achieve instant enlightenment. Only mobilize this true interest and there will be no distinction between a straw hut and a palace of gold. If we allow passion to blind us, then we will lose much of the beauty of life.

46. The achievement of virtue and the cultivation of the way require a will as steady and firm as a tree or rock. Once one becomes enamored of the glittering splendor of the outside world, then that is to descend into desire; governing the state and helping the people requires a sense as simple as clouds and water. Once there is avarice and corruption then that is to plunge into danger.

Entangled in the bustle of the red dust of the mundane world, one is within an inch of the hounds of temptation. The ancients said: "Pretty lips and moth-like brows are the axe that hews both character and spirit." Once people abandon themselves to the intoxication of a life of luxury and forget the way back, then both body and mind will suffer serious injury. Thus, the gentleman of wisdom in cultivating his character requires a will of stones and trees, unmoved by desire; those in high positions require a will of clouds and water, unaffected and at ease. Once the train of desire sets out, it is on the rails of no return and bound for the eternal abyss.

47. *The upright man is calm in word and deed and brims with goodwill even in his dreams; the man of violence is evil in conduct and even his laughter is muddy with murderous intent.*

Inner moral character can express itself through external speech and action. It is because of this that the Chinese people have always sought to "watch one's words and gestures." It is by the minute observation of facial expression and its changes that one may come to understand and discriminate amongst people and thus actively draw close to gentlemen and consciously shun rogues.

48. If the liver is sick then the eyes cannot see, if the kidneys are sick then the ears cannot hear. Illness takes hold unseen but appears for all to see. Thus, the gentleman who does not wish to offend in public must first not give offence in private.

The Confucians believed that a cultivated gentleman should above all act with sincerity and honesty. It is easy to present an appearance of honesty and urbanity in public but far more difficult to maintain unanimity of behavior in private. The nature and quality of someone's moral conduct will only be apparent in all its reality when he is alone. Consequently, the Confucians emphasized the idea that: "The gentleman should exercise prudence in private." Cultivating a virtuous character must start from the state of privacy. It is only by truly putting effort into prudence in private that one can achieve an openhearted sincerity and justness of mind.

49. Man has no greater joy than unhurried leisure and no greater disaster than anxiety and suspicion. Only the bitterly busy can know the joy of leisure and only the even-tempered can begin to know the calamity of anxiety and suspicion.

The ancient proverb says: "Good fortune is easy to seek but leisure is difficult to enjoy." Worldly riches, honor, fame and profit have been sought after and hoped for by many. A little may be gained through great effort and struggle and life may be lived in prosperity and good health. Nevertheless, however great one's good fortune its anxieties are difficult to dispel. Every aspect of life becomes tiring and involved and people are fatigued through wasting much of the beauty of life by rushing about. The Song dynasty (960–1279) poet Su Shi (1037–1101) said: "The finest flavor of life is leisure." Life's most invaluable quality is the sweet flavor of leisure. It is in a leisurely mood that one can take the time to experience the beauty of tranquility and peace.

50. Be square and upright in the ordered world but round and crafty in the chaotic world. In the last days of a collapsing world be both square and round. Be generous in the treatment of the virtuous and severe in the treatment of the wicked. In the treatment of the generality of people be both generous and severe.

In one's conduct in society there is no absolute black or white, right or wrong, good or evil. One must act on the basis of the characteristics of one's opponent, adjusting one's manner of dealing with people and things. In this way, no matter whether one is situated in ordered prosperity or chaos, or dealing with the virtuous or the wicked, it becomes as easy as cutting a knife through butter and one is invincible.

51. If I make a contribution to others, that is not a matter for concern, if I treat others badly, that is a matter of deep concern; if others benefit me, I should never forget, if they complain of me, then I cannot but forget.

If we treat others badly, we should reflect upon it and remember and if there is an opportunity, make it up to them, only then can our conscience be stilled and our sleep untroubled. The ancients said: "A single drop of benevolence should be repaid with a torrent." No matter whether it is just a single drop, it should be engraved on our heart and the benevolence repaid with virtue. Friction always occurs in relationships and provided the parameters of the relationship are unaffected one should be magnanimous and treasure harmony above all. Treat people well, harbor a sense of gratitude and society will be filled with the warmth of harmony.

52. The benevolent man does not see himself as such, nor does he regard his beneficiary as an object of charity, thus even a pinch of benevolence may receive a return in sincerity of many times its value; those who openly advantage and favor others not only flaunt their generosity but require gratitude in return, though they may lay out gold by the ton they hardly receive a copper coin's worth of value in return.

Laozi said: "Virtue should be like the water that nurtures all living things but does not seek a name for itself." This kind of undemanding, unforced attitude to behavior in society seems to display a state of sublimity, like the flow of a multitude of rivers. Only the spirit of such a state can win hearts. It imbues a person with a gentle, subdued approach that will gain the respect and support of the common man. If you always help others in the expectation of a return, you are selfishly corrupting virtue. You are not doing good works but indulging in a business transaction.

53. Opportunity and circumstance are both favorable and unfavorable, how can one ensure that they favor oneself? The moods of man too are both favorable and unfavorable, how can they all be made favorable to oneself? To be able to reflect upon and manage this is a door on the path to enlightenment.

The life of man is both smooth and stony, both calm and undisturbed, both tempestuous and sun scorched. Man's moods rise and fall in confusing change between happiness and anger, joy and sorrow. More often than not, things do not go the way one wishes and there is little joy in one's heart. The harshness of fate is a commonplace of life. Consequently, one must face the storms of life in a calm and composed frame of mind. Once settled in mind and spirit, the trials and tribulations of life appear as not necessarily a scene of gloom and desolation.

54. Only when pure in heart and mind may one learn and study from the past. Otherwise virtuous deeds may be appropriated for one's own help and words of virtue plagiarized to conceal one's own shortcomings. This is to supply weapons to the enemy and food to bandits.

One of the poems of the Tang dynasty (618–907) poet Du Fu (712–770) has the line: "Virtue rules when the wise are noble." That is—not all those filled with learning are of good character. History has more than a few characters of great wickedness, the more talented they were, the greater the damage they wreaked. The Qing dynasty educational work, *Rules for Children and Pupils* says: "Where there is effort to spare it should be devoted to learning"—once one has mastered the morality of one's own thinking, surplus energy should go towards further study and enquiry. The primary task of education in the eyes of the ancients was the nurture of good moral character. Further study of the classics and an increase in knowledge was on the basis of respect for the old and love for the young, deference and honesty together with compassion and the desire to be worthy. Consequently, in learning and scholarship, heart and mind must be pure and virtuous. Talent is second to virtue. When virtue controls talent, it can become genius; talent without virtue is crooked and mediocre.

55. The extravagant may be rich yet never have enough, how can they emulate the thrifty who achieve abundance in poverty? The able toil but provoke hatred, how can they emulate the clumsy who are yet at ease in themselves?

The agricultural society of ancient China shaped one of China's most valuable assets, an admirable sense of frugality. The Tang dynasty poet, Li Shangyin (c.813–c.858) said: "Observe the worthy states and families of the past, how they rose by frugal toil and fell by extravagance." A life of luxury is not necessarily bad but once desire takes hold, a life of the utmost luxury cannot fill the emptiness of the heart. If one expends every device of heart and mind in the acquisition of wealth and position by fair means or foul, its acquisition is of no significance. Standing in the midst of the frantic search for favor and the pursuit of fame and profit, there are many enemies, bringing with them exclusion and revenge. How can this life of sweetness poised at the knife's edge compare with that of honest people who live in truth and simplicity? The frugal life has its own delights.

56. To study but not to perceive the essence of virtue is to be like the printer who merely applies ink; to govern but not to perceive the wants of the people is to be like a thief clad in official costume. To hold forth but not to implement the meaning is merely to pay lip service to truth; to establish a business but not to consider planting the seeds of morality is to resemble a bunch of withered flowers.

The purpose of learning is both for the refinement of one's nature and the study of a practical application. Study should see past the superficiality of words to touch the true essence of the sages. An official should not turn his back on the people but benefit them. The ancients described those who governed as "mother-father officials." Parents love their own children above all and an official must cherish his people as parents love their children. He must regard serving the people as an expression of the worth of his own life before there can be any long-lasting achievement. Merely seeking prestige and benefit for oneself and ignoring the desires of the people is an achievement like a cactus that flowers only at night, a mere flash in the darkness.

57. The heart of man contains a single true essay but it is obscured by tattered fragments; it has one true music but it is drowned out by songs of sorcery and erotic dances. The scholar must sweep away the influences of the outer world to find the original truth before there can be any true benefit.

The Confucians advocated: "Preserve the principles of heaven, extinguish the desires of men," the Daoists believed that: "The Way is of and in the Natural World," and the Buddhists emphasized: "Illuminate the heart and see one's nature." One can see from this that Confucianism, Daoism and Buddhism, the traditional philosophies of China, all considered that in the beginning the nature of man was virtuous but that it had been corrupted by layer upon layer of subsequent desire to the point where it had changed beyond recognition. Consequently, Confucian self-cultivation comprised the concept of "illumine the bright virtue"— causing the brightness of man's original virtuous nature to shine forth once more; Daoist practice emphasized "a return to infancy"—returning to a state of childhood innocence; Buddhist self-cultivation sought a return to the "original appearance"—the constant sweeping away of the dust of desire, anger and ignorance. It is only by abandoning the deceptions of material desire and returning to the original starting point of the uncorrupted soul that we can transcend the mundane, become a Buddha and achieve in life.

58. The suffering heart often contains a hint of joy but satisfaction can breed disappointment.

The Confucians say: "Wisdom to the utmost but follow the Middle Way." In all life's circumstances, whether easy or hard, in joy or in grief, one should not adhere to one particular side but deal with things in an evenhanded way. As one puts painstaking effort into the pursuit of an aim, one should snatch a moment of leisure from the midst of toil, a moment of joy from sorrow, so that tension and relaxation are in balance and so that taking and giving can be exercised freely. One should be particularly careful at the moment of successful achievement to prevent tragedy springing from joy and bad from good.

*59. Riches and reputation derived from virtue grow
slowly and unforced, like the flowers of the forest; if
they derive from achievement they are like flowers
in a pot, always in danger of being moved or thrown
away; if they derive from power they are like rootless
flowers in a vase, they cannot grow and can only stand
and wither.*

There are three ways to riches, reputation and the
enjoyment of wealth and position: through morality,
through achievement and through power. *Zuo's Commentary
on the Spring and Autumn Annals*, a famous work of Chinese
historiography says: "At the very summit stands morality,
then achievement and then words,"—if a gentleman seeks
to win an untarnished reputation, it is first established
through morality, next through achievement and finally
through writing and the establishment of theory. Wealth
and position won through morality last the longest; that
won by achievement contains many variables; that won by
power may disappear in the blink of an eye. Wealth and
position are, of course, a beautiful aspiration. The crux of
the matter is whether or not you have the deserved good
fortune to be able to control them.

60. Spring arrives softly, flowers spread in color and birds warble in song. Yet if gentleman scholars of outstanding talent, warm and well-fed once more, think not of fine words or virtuous acts, though they may live a hundred years, it seems as if they have lived not a day.

As we live this life, apart from individualism we must make a contribution to others, otherwise it is a life lived in vain. The Tang dynasty poet, Li Bai (701–762) said: "Heaven gave me talent. It must have some value." If spring flowers can adorn the beauty of the world and birds in spring offer the beauty of their song, then how much more can scholars with a bellyful of talent offer? If a person of sensibility, with wind in his sails and possessed of outstanding talent writes nothing of value and does nothing good, it is a betrayal of heaven and an insult to self.

61. The scholar requires a prudent mind but also a sense of the unconventional. To be restrained in misery by self is like death in autumn rather than birth in spring, how then may all sentient beings flourish?

Scholarship obviously requires diligence and effort but it should not, because of this, resemble an ascetic monk who has reduced himself to a state of total lifelessness. Apart from diligence and application there should also be a sense of the enjoyment of life. To turn oneself into a pool of stagnant water, where then is the enthusiasm and warmth that can enrich the lives of others and bring warmth to the world as a whole?

62. The truly honest do not seek a name for honesty, those that establish such a name for themselves are fishing for fame; the wise do not flaunt their wisdom, those that do, do so to conceal their stupidity.

The Daoist philosophical work *Daodejing* says: "The honest appear crooked and the ingenious appear clumsy." The upright man may seem easygoing and the wise man may appear simple. The incorruptible man has no need to advertise his incorruptibility; the wise man has no need to win fame through cunning trickery. Cheating may win a moment but will lose a lifetime in the end.

63. A water ewer may tip when full and a money box split when crammed. Hence the gentleman would rather live in detachment than engagement and in insufficiency rather than sufficiency.

The *Book of Changes* explains the way of change. Almost each one of its 64 divinatory hexagrams forecasts evil in the midst of good and vice versa. There is only a single exception that is entirely good; this is the trigram *qian*—modesty. Water when full, spills; man when full of himself, falls. A man puffed up with arrogant self-satisfaction will finally tip over to destruction like an overfilled ewer. The gentleman of wisdom will conduct himself modestly and prudently, leave space for others in all things and not seek to secure all advantage to himself.

*64. Those who have not pulled up the roots of fame,
though they may despise wealth and position and
willingly live a simple life, will always fall prey to the
passions of the secular world; those who cannot absorb
and transmute the influences of the outside world,
though their benevolence may fill the four seas and
benefit endless ages, in the end that benevolence will be
mere superfluous trickery.*

This flourishing world is limitless in its extent. Without
the will to stand aside it is impossible to abandon
attachment to fame and profit. There are people who
distance themselves from the red dust, their spirit
dwelling with hills and water and at ease amongst forests
and springs, who cannot break this attachment to fame
and profit. It matters not how noble they may appear,
that affinity for mud remains in their bones, its vulgarity
reaching the heavens.

65. An openhearted man is like the blue sky in a darkened room; dark thoughts are like devils in daylight.

The three philosophies of China—Confucianism, Daoism and Buddhism—all emphasize the bright purity of man's heart. Kindness of heart can illuminate even the darkest of rooms in which we may find ourselves but deceit and treachery will seem as if malign spirits are abroad on even the finest days. With Buddha in the heart all will seem Buddhas. If there are demons in the heart then every sentient being is a demon. The external world you see is a projection of your own inner heart.

66. Man knows the joy of fame and position but not the true joy of neither fame nor position; man knows the suffering of hunger and cold but not the deeper suffering of neither hunger nor cold.

Daoism emphasizes that "have and have not, with and without are born of each other." If life is to be complete, there must also be loss as well as gain. In society today, however, we are only aware of the joy of "with." We enjoy the success of "gain" and find it difficult to comprehend the existence of "without" or to accept the regret of "loss." Life is not all bouquets and applause; we should be able to enjoy its bustle and excitement but should also enjoy the ordinary and the peaceful. Irrespective of fame and position we should live our lives in happiness and joy.

*67. To do harm but fear that others may know, then
the way to virtue still exists within one's wickedness;
to do good but to be anxious that others should know,
then evil is already rooted in the good.*

The nature of man is complicated and changeable, there
is both good and evil. The evil-minded person who,
in performing an evil deed still fears to be found out,
demonstrates that he retains a sense of right and wrong
and realizes that he has committed a crime. Those who
commit evil but do not care are truly sunk in degradation.
Those who do a little good but are anxious to advertise it
have a heart shriveled in the smoke of profit and desire.
The concept of present benefit will be the cause of their
later ruin.

68. The motions of heaven are unfathomable, backwards and forwards, now benign now malign, playing tricks on the heroes of humanity. The gentleman should accept adversity calmly and though living in peace, have a care for danger, thus heaven will be powerless to employ its trickery.

The proverb goes: "The weather of the heavens cannot be foretold; man has disaster and fortune both day and night." Life is not perpetual ease and convenience but the hardships and obstructions on the way do not last forever. Confucius said: "Act to the utmost of one's ability but heed the will of heaven." One's external environment is always in a state of flux, so one's own will should be as solid as a rock. Meet the challenges of fate with an unyielding will and even if you were the Creator himself, what could be done about it?

69. The choleric man is like a flame that burns all it encounters; the mean-minded man is like ice that freezes you to death. The stupidly obstinate man is like stagnant water or rotten wood, his life force extinguished. They are all incapable of achievement or wellbeing.

As you strive for achievement and happiness in life there are three kinds of people to be avoided. The first is the hot-tempered man who will burn you to ash; the second is the man as unfeeling as a block of ice who will freeze the soul out of you; the third is the inflexibly obstinate man who will squeeze the life out of you so that you lose all interest. These three lack the ability to achieve or to reap the reward of happiness.

70. Happiness cannot be sought deliberately, it is a matter of nurturing an outlook that attracts happiness; disaster may be unavoidable, it is a matter of ridding oneself of the instinct to do harm.

Happiness may be very fine but there is no need to set one's mind on seeking it. One only needs to maintain a positive and optimistic frame of mind, rather as if a god of happiness dwelt in one's own heart, and happiness will follow you every step of the way; disaster is disagreeable but cannot be banished by scheming it away. Ridding oneself of the instinct to harm others would be like donning a protective suit that keeps away calamity and repels disaster.

*71. To speak well nine out of ten times will not
necessarily attract praise but to speak badly once will
be considered a crime; nine out of ten schemes may
succeed but there may be no approval, let one scheme
fail and criticism will be rife. Hence the gentleman
should be silent rather than loquacious and clumsy
rather than agile.*

In the theory of the making of tubs, the heights of the
staves that make up the tub are not all the same and it is
the shortest stave that determines how much water the tub
will hold. Life is confusing and jealousies abound. People
do not look at the long staves in a tub but concentrate on
the short one. People will not praise you for your many
successes but will, in ceaseless criticism, concentrate their
gaze on your defects and shortcomings. The gentleman of
cultivation must be careful in speech and action and avoid
rash impetuosity on the basis of a moment's pleasure,
thereby providing a hook upon which others may hang
their criticism.

72. In the weather of this world, warmth brings life and cold kills. Thus, it is that those of a frigid disposition are equally cold in their enjoyment; only the kind and warmhearted will enjoy abundant happiness and long-lasting favor.

In dealing with the world one should treat others with the warmth and splendor of spring and summer to give them warmth and hope, rather than treat them with the cold desolation of autumn and winter to bring them destruction, fear, and despair. The Confucian classic *Mengzi* says: "Those that love their fellow men will always be loved in return, those that respect their fellow men will always be respected in return." Those that love gain a return of love, those that spread happiness will gather it. To hold love in oneself and to love and respect others will garner their love and respect for you.

73. The path of heavenly principle is broad, travel but a little way along it and one feels its vast magnificence; the track of man's desire is narrow, set out upon it and it is all brambles and mud.　＼

Zhu Xi (1130–1200), the great neo-Confucian philosopher of the Rationalist School of the Song dynasty, considered that the ideal moral state involved the elimination of selfish desire and the opening of the mind to the expression of its original radiantly pure moral integrity. This proposition became the banner of the Confucian ideal of the cultivation of mind and body. To indulge in selfish desire and to allow the intellect to be blinded by lust is to set out on a narrow, dangerous path of no return. One can only sigh at the fact that from the past to the present so few people have been visible on the path of heavenly principle while the path of desire is so crowded.

74. Hardship and joy both temper one's character, practice to the utmost and happiness will be long-lasting; doubt and belief constitute the process of enquiry, enquire to the utmost and the wisdom acquired will be both true and pure.

Life is not all sunlight and warmth; there is wind and rain as well. Only a baptism of wind and rain can consolidate true and long-lasting happiness. It is the same principle with study and scholarship. Texts must be believed and acknowledged but they must also be doubted and questioned. An acceptable truth can only be achieved through the discovery that the intellectual propositions will stand up to rigorous scholarly scrutiny. Otherwise, "It is better to be without books than to believe in them absolutely." Where is the interest in blind belief and superficial knowledge?

75. *The mind must be unoccupied and tranquil to accommodate learning, but solid to resist material desire.*

In the practice of self-cultivation, one should, on the one hand, clear one's head of subjective prejudice and be open to the truth; on the other hand, one should maintain a substantial and immoveable state of mind capable of resisting material desire. Be unoccupied and tranquil when required, otherwise there will be no room for the truth; be solid when solidity is needed and present no opportunity to material desire.

76. The dirt of the earth produces living things; clean water often lacks fish. Hence the gentleman should accept a measure of dirt and not adopt an attitude of solitary purity.

The excrement of animals is filthy but it is the best manure for plants; distilled water is pure and clean but of no nourishment for the human body. A person who stands too aloof will separate himself from the world and be unable to promote the growth of living things. A gentleman must have a measure of tolerance for a rogue. To be different but in harmony and in a large measure tolerant of the mundane world, that is the best mental venue for self-cultivation.

77. *The fiercest horse may be trained to gallop, metal spilled in smelting will still fit the mold. Ease and idleness will never bring progress. Master Chen Xianzhang said: "Defects in behavior are no matter for shame, it is the blameless life that concerns me." This is a truth indeed.*

As we live in this world, there should be no fear of individuality or of doing things wrong, if we adjust our nature we can achieve much. If we fear, we should fear that there are people who appear foursquare and steady and without defects but who are mediocre and ordinary and will never achieve anything.

78. A moment of selfish thought and strength turns weak, wisdom becomes stupidity, kindness turns cruel and purity is infected with filth to the destruction of one's character for life. Hence the ancients treasured selflessness as the quality of a lifetime.

The Buddhist *Essay on Contrition* says: "All past evil arose from greed, anger and ignorance." Greed is the principal enemy of self-cultivation. Once greed has taken root in the heart, a man will be drawn in by selfish desire, his head will be turned by greed and he will become weak, stupid, cruel and corrupt. The treasure of selflessness, however, will last a lifetime.

79. Ears, eyes, sight and sound are the thieves without,
lust and sensuality the thieves within. As long as
the master of the house is alert and clearheaded and
remains upright and principled the thieves may be
turned to family.

In Buddhist lore, there are six internal roots: eyes, the root
of sight; ears, the root of sound; nose, the root of smell;
tongue, the root of taste; body the root of touch; mind, the
root of thought. There are also six external "dusts"—color,
sound, scent, taste, touch and awareness—the latter being
the consciousness of the characteristics of the previous
five. Self-cultivation is the cleansing of the six roots so that
they are not contaminated by a single grain of dust. The
six roots are termed internal desires while the six dusts
are external temptations and they are the deadly enemy of
practice. The rigorous watch over, and prevention of each
wayward thought rather resembles the master of the house
presiding in the hall while neither the restlessly stirring
inner thieves or the enticing outer thieves move an inch
and meekly transform themselves, root and branch, into
congenial and lovable members of the family.

80. It is better to preserve past achievement than to seek future merit; it is better to prevent future wrongs than regret past mistakes.

Life has only three days: yesterday, today and tomorrow. Yesterday has already gone; tomorrow is yet to come. Only today is left to live well. It is better to work steadily at the task of the moment than to harbor illusions of future glory. It is only today that is within your grasp: better to consider how to avoid tomorrow's mistakes than repent yesterday's errors, for the key to self-improvement lies in the here and now.

81. One's comportment should be vast and lofty yet not tempestuous; thought should be meticulous but not petty; one's tastes should be moderate but not insipid; one's conduct should be firm but not intense.

Everybody today wants to be the perfect gentleman but finds it difficult to grasp the rules for being so. To conduct oneself well requires a certain lack of restraint but if overdone this easily turns to an overbearing impetuosity. The handling of affairs requires a meticulous mind, but overdone this easily becomes a troublesome interest in the merely trivial. You may strive for an elegant simplicity but you should not be too interested in enjoying the fragrance of one's own reputation. You may conduct yourself with care and caution but you should not become excessively narrow-minded. Having a grasp that does not incline too far one way or the other, being refined to the point of perfection, that is the epitome of the sense of the quotation from one of the classic Confucian *Four Books*, *Doctrine of the Mean*: "Strive for brilliance but keep to the Middle Way." Put your effort into achieving a state of lofty radiance and make impartiality part of the art of self-cultivation.

82. The wind comes and soughs amongst the bamboos, it leaves and no sound remains; the wild goose flies across the cold pool, it leaves and its shadow disappears. The mind of a gentleman takes notice when something occurs; once over, the mind is void again.

The Buddhist *Diamond Sutra* says: "The mind should be free of attachment and not dwell in a single state." This is the very summit state of self-improvement. Events occur and you deal with them in a calm and natural manner, but without forming an attachment and without being ensnared by the external state. Not to react to events is to be utterly lifeless like a pool of stagnant water; still to be entangled after the event is to fall into delusion, stupidity and obsession. Do not fend off events but do not hang on to them.

83. Purity may be tolerant, humanity may be decisive, minute enquiry may not be excessive and the truth should not be carried too far. This is to say that honey is not too sweet to use or the sea too salty; that is true virtue.

The reason that Confucians emphasize the Middle Way is so that conduct in society should be appropriate, leaning neither one way nor the other. The honest and upright man, whilst upholding righteousness, should do so both magnanimously and gently so as to avoid over-correction and extremes of behavior. Charitable people should be firm and decisive in their dealings to prevent kindness of heart blinding common sense. People who are strict and impartial may well enquire and investigate minutely but should not be over-critical. The just man is upright but not fiercely unbending. The finest way of conducting oneself is to have a firm grasp of the rules of the Middle Way.

84. Poor families sweep the ground clean, poor women have combs in their hair, their surroundings may not be splendid but their demeanor is elegant. How then can the gentleman situated in dull loneliness give up and abandon all?

The ancients said, "A man may be poor but his will is not impoverished." A family's material life may be one of respectable destitution but they can still appear spick and span; the frugal man may still appear neatly dressed, such families and such people are worthy of respect. Material deficiency is not genuine poverty, circumstances may be improved by effort and struggle; it is spiritual frustration and disappointment that is the true poverty, it saps the will and causes people to give up in despair. The gentleman of ability, even if he is ill situated, must still retain his ideals and ambitions and optimistically push on upwards.

85. In leisure do not toss time away, take enjoyment when busy; do not let tranquility slip past, reap the benefits of activity; in darkness do not seek to do evil but accept the benefits of light.

Do not waste one's leisure, be unhurried when busy. Tao Kan (259–334) the great minister of the Eastern Jin dynasty (317–420) did not lose heart when exiled to the wilds as a local official but carried bricks back and forth to exercise his body so that if the state needed him again he would be fit to take office once more. It is better to be still rather than active but calm should not be allowed to lapse into empty dreams. One may profit greatly from activity but depend upon calm in which to gather one's thoughts. "If you do not perform shameful deeds during the day, you will not fear the knock on the door at night." Do not perform acts that offend the conscience when out of sight, only then will you be able to face others openly and with a clear conscience. One night, one of the underlings of the Eastern Han dynasty minister Yang Zhen (?–124), attempted to make him a gift of money which he refused. The underling said: "The night is dark, nobody will know." Yang Zhen replied: "Heaven knows, the earth knows, you know and I know, how can you say that nobody knows?"

86. When a thought surfaces and you realize that it will take the path of desire, you must wrest it back on to the path of principle. To realize at the start and to turn away once you realize, that is how to turn from disaster to fortune. It is the moment to turn back to life from death, do not let it slip by.

Cultivation of the mind is the essence of practice. Of itself, the mind is fundamentally pure but the functions of the mind are part Buddha part demon. When heavenly principle illuminates, then Buddha is in the hall, when thoughts of desire stir, demons occupy the mind. Distraction is not to be feared but tardiness of realization is. The moment one discovers that the mind is sliding towards the path of desire, then that is the time to drag it on to the path of principle. Leave the mind unguarded, indulge in desire and it opens the way to the approach of destruction and the arrival of catastrophe. One must be alert and vigilant the whole time, never ruin one's whole life for a moment of ecstasy.

87. *With tranquility comes clarity of mind, when one can perceive its true substance; in leisure, the quality of the mind is calm and one may know the deep motions of the heart; in mildness, interests are harmonious and one may gain the true flavor of the heart. In observing heart and mind one may comprehend the supreme principle of enlightenment. There is nothing better than these three states of mind.*

There are three direct routes to the self-examination of mind and the comprehension of sacred principle: first, the maintenance of a calm state of mind that allows distractions to settle, this is the core of the innate quality of the mind; second, to maintain a mood of unhurried calm that allows the innate qualities of the mind to shine upon all living things, this is the deep motion of the mind; finally, to maintain a sense of simplicity that allows the mind a contented freedom, this is the true flavor of the mind.

88. The calm of tranquility is not true calm, the calm won from activity is its natural state; joy of itself is not true joy, the joy gained through suffering is the only true motion of the mind itself.

What is real tranquility? Relaxedly sitting and reading is not real tranquility. Real tranquility is the ability to relax and read surrounded by the noise of a market place because you have a mind that is never disturbed by external interference. What is real joy? Excited chatter in a luxurious setting is not real joy, since once the performance is over the crowd disperses and loneliness will take over again. Real happiness and joy derive from living positively and optimistically in a difficult environment.

89. Selflessness should not be self-interested, if it is, the selfless aims become shameful; charity should not seek reward, if it does, benevolent intentions turn to naught.

In doing good works do not scheme for an outcome. It will lead to hesitation and will cover your original benevolent intentions with shame. Do not seek reward when helping others. If you do so you will corrupt your own wish to help others. To scheme and reckon profit and loss and to seek reward shows that you have not entirely rid yourself of your attachment to "me," everything revolves round it. On the surface you may appear to be helping others, in fact you are both selfish and self-seeking at heart.

90. Heaven is miserly with the happiness it bestows upon me but I am generous in the virtue with which I receive it; heaven wearies my body with labor, I ease my heart to compensate for it; heaven puts misfortune in my way, I prepare my mind to comprehend it. How can heaven treat me thus?

The *Mengzi* says: "When heaven wishes to place a great task upon somebody, it first causes him suffering of mind, wearies his bones, starves his body, impoverishes his state and obstructs his work, thus strengthening his character and adding to the abilities that he lacked hitherto." A man wishing to do great things must undergo hardship and temper himself amidst difficulty and adversity and win victory through an unyielding will. Heaven tests us by being miserly with happiness, by fatiguing our bodies and putting suffering in our way, yet this is an opportunity as well. As long as you face this positively, you will reap an abundant harvest.

91. The true gentleman has no appetite for the acquisition of good fortune, but heaven will fathom his inner feelings; the lesser man is careful to avoid disaster but heaven will steal away his soul. Thus, one can perceive the wonder and power of the motions of heaven; of what profit then are the mere shifts and contrivances of man?

Outwardly, matters of life and death, riches and position are determined by heaven, but in reality, they are the inspirations of self. Whether or not heaven visits you with riches or disaster depends, in the main, upon what causes you have set in train. The auspicious man is not minded to seek fortune but fortune comes rolling in, the lesser man is careful to avoid disaster but disaster follows at his heels. This is the wonder of the motions of heaven. How pitiful is the genius of man!

92. The virtues of a courtesan of renown who follows the path of righteousness in later life are not obscured by her dubious previous life; for the chaste lady who suffers infirmity in her old age, the upright suffering of early life counts as nothing. Truly it is said: "To know a man, know only his life's latter half."

In their judgment of men, the ancients placed great importance upon the later years, seeking a proper conclusion to life. A failure of conduct in later life would attract criticism. There have been people who achieved much when young but later fell by the wayside of indulgence and these faults became a stain upon their lives as a whole. Others abandoned a dissipated youth and turned over a new leaf in later life, and because of their return to righteousness from evil they gained the sympathy of the public.

93. Commoners who exercise virtue and bestow benevolence are ministers without office; officials who pursue power and seek favor are just beggars with a title.

Commoners or aristocracy, those who possess a fine spiritual character will also have charm and charisma and win the approval and support of others. Those who hunger after power and position and lack any scruples are without character and despite any wealth they may have accumulated, will be spurned by all. People of truly good character, however ordinary they may be, will earn the love, respect, and praise of all.

94. Ask what benefit flows from our ancestors, it is all that we now enjoy, thus we should consider the difficulty of its accumulation; ask what enriches our progeny, it is all that we bequeath, thus we should consider the ease of its dispersal.

It is difficult to build a great building but it can collapse in the twinkling of an eye. The good atmosphere in a family is inseparable from the transmitted traditions of generations of ancestors. As we live in the world, we should treat the family with a deep feeling of responsibility and demand of ourselves that we should pass on good family customs, and that we should also set a good example for our children, grandchildren and later generations.

95. The feigned virtue of the gentleman is no different from the wanton wickedness of the rogue; the altered conduct of a gentleman is not better than the self-reform of the rogue.

A gentleman is a person of refined character who is moral, upright and honest. If he is not truly virtuous and obtains his good name by cheating then he is a false gentleman. The false gentleman may appear noble and upright with an outward air of elegance but in truth he is hypocritical, false, inconsistent, unscrupulous, and utterly without moral basis. He is more loathsome than a rogue. The rogue is easy to hide from but the false gentleman is difficult to avoid. In this world of falsehood, let us behave like true gentlemen.

96. Do not be swift to anger against a family member who has erred but do not ignore it, such matters are difficult to speak of and should be approached by way of a different example; if they do not comprehend today, wait until another day to warn them once more. The model family is one where the spring winds thaw the ice and the warmth melts it.

The most difficult form of education and cultivation takes place within close relationships. Within the family it is important to be tolerant and when mistakes are made, to resolve them like the spring wind melting snow. Rushing headlong into criticism and abuse or waging an uncaring cold war will turn the warmth of paradise to a frozen hell. If the family is harmonious all will be well. One should see things from the other point of view and treasure the affection within the family.

97. When the heart is full, the world beneath heaven will be without flaw; when the heart is open all beneath heaven will be free of evil.

Whether you see the world as perfect or a matter for regret, safe or sinister, that is a projection of your inner mind. When your mind is full of beauty and overflowing with love and you look at the world, its multitudinous defects no longer exist; if your mind is filled with tolerance and peace and you look at the world again you will see that the workings and relationships of the world are no longer sinister. Let us look at the world with hearts filled with beauty. I see how beautiful the world is and hope that the world will look on me in the same way. The world and man, joined in joy.

98. The man of sober tastes is an object of suspicion to lovers of the magnificent; the frugal man is shunned by the wanton. In these circumstances, the gentleman can neither alter his conduct nor display his abilities!

Jealousy and suspicion are common in personal relationships. In our conduct in society we may not be able to change our environment but we can improve ourselves. We may not be able to root out jealousy and suspicion from human nature but we can protect ourselves with wisdom. In the company of rogues, strong in suspicion and heavy with jealousy, we need to be reserved rather than expansive in order to avoid baseless suspicion and frenzied slander.

99. Situated in adversity, we are surrounded by the whetstones upon which to hone morality, and do so unaware; situated in favorable circumstances our eyes are filled by the sight of weapons that dissolve the flesh and grind the bones without our knowing.

Circumstances of hardship and difficulty have always been able to stimulate the will to survive, unconsciously honing the will and tempering morality in the process of the struggle upwards. In circumstances of wealth and leisure it is very easy to give way to the indulgences that lead to corruption and depravity. "From ancient times heroes have been tempered by adversity, heroes have rarely sprung from the ranks of the gilded youth." A life of comfort is not the birthplace of valiant heroes. Consequently, we should not fear difficulty or adversity but face the challenges of life with confidence and optimism.

100. Growing up in the homes of the rich and noble, lust is a fierce fire and power a burning flame. Without a sense of restraint, the flames may not devour others but will consume self.

The Daoist philosophical classic *Daodejing* says: "None may keep safe a hall filled with gold and jade. The pride of riches and honor brings its own calamity." However much money you may have, it is difficult to protect; becoming arrogant on account of wealth and honor will bring disaster. Living amongst wealth and honor requires self-restraint more than ever. Indulgence in lust, no matter how much wealth and power you possess, will cause you to be utterly consumed by the flames of desire so that not a single bone remains. The rewards of happiness should be treasured and not squandered recklessly. When the overdraft of halcyon days comes to an end, hard days follow.

101. When the heart of man is honest, frost may form in summer, city walls may fall and flint may be carved; when the heart is false, man is nothing but a dead soul, a skeleton in a skin, loathsome in the sight of others and shameful to himself.

The proverb says: "The honest heart can split metal." A man whose heart is true can move heaven and earth so that even the hardest metal or stone can be split asunder. Chinese mythology has it that Zou Yan (c. 305–240 BC), a philosopher of the period of the Warring States, was unjustly imprisoned and that heaven sent frost in the heat of summer to signal the injustice that he had suffered. The husband of Meng Jiangnü died through the cruelty of forced labor and she wept bitterly at the foot of the Great Wall, causing it to collapse suddenly. Thus, the true and honest heart has unimaginable strength. The falsehearted rogue will always be shunned, even if he can manipulate power and gain momentary satisfaction.

102. There is nothing strange about the well-expressed essay, it is just right and nothing else; there is nothing unusual about the well-developed character, it is as it was in the beginning and no more.

The great Tang dynasty poet Li Bai said that the highest realms of literature were like "hibiscus flowers in clear water, an adornment of nature." Well-written works are like lotus flowers in a pool, naturally beautiful and completely unaffected. Nevertheless, writers love ornate rhetoric, seeking a particular stylistic skill that can show off their talents and abilities. This kind of artificial writing lacks the ability to move the heart. One's conduct is the same; a deliberate display of ostentatious novelty to attract attention is a last desperate attempt to survive. The truly able have no need of deliberate mystification; it is just a case of returning to one's true original nature and of openhearted, natural simplicity.

103. In the state of illusion, not only fame, wealth and position but one's very body and limbs are bestowed by heaven; in the state of reality, not only mother and father and brothers but all living things are as one body. Only by seeing through to the truth can man assume the burden of heaven and throw off the shackles of the world.

Buddhism teaches us that in the origin of things one's nature was void and that all phenomena and living things arose from a combination of various causes and that those, too, were inherently void. Consequently, one has to be able to see through and be able to relinquish. One's body was formed through a process of transformation; how much more so the non-corporeal qualities of fame, wealth and position? Looked at another way, all phenomena and living things are formed from different causes. However, since they possess an external existence, they must be capable of being assumed as a burden and of being recognized in truth, thus one should treasure mother, father and brothers and cherish all the living things of heaven and earth. If you can see through, then you can live unencumbered in freedom; if you can recognize in truth, then you can assume the heavy burdens of heaven.

104. Flavors that delight the mouth are as a herb that rots the guts and decays the bones, just take as a half and disaster will be prevented; matters that please the heart are as a substance that does ill to the body and weakens morality, just take as a half and shame will be avoided.

Many illnesses are the result of the urge for comfort eating and of eating and drinking without restraint. So today, fine dining should be undertaken with suitable restraint thus avoiding illness. The same principle applies in the conduct of affairs. The unrestrained and impetuous enjoyment of pleasurable experience can leave a reputation in tatters and cause long-lasting regret.

*105. Do not condemn small faults, do not spread
shameful secrets, and do not dwell on past wrongs.
These three rules will nurture virtue and put harm
at a distance.*

Giving a little more space to others means a few more
friends; a little less grievance means fewer enemies. There
are some people in our daily life who expect perfection
and are over-particular about the faults of others, even
going as far as deliberately revealing their shortcomings
and cataloguing their faults. It is not realized that this will
not only fail to achieve any good result but will set people
against each other and breed hatred between them. In
social conduct it is harmony in relationships that should be
valued. A life of happiness is only possible if you have the
capacity to maintain an optimistic frame of mind and to
treat others well.

106. The gentleman should not approach the practice of self-restraint lightly, if he does, the material world will encroach upon the self and it will be deprived of ease and calm; the gentleman should not become too deeply involved, if he does, the self will be mired in the material world and it will be deprived of the chance to rise above the mundane.

The gentleman should do his utmost to cultivate an attitude of dignified calm. If he treats people lightly and affairs impetuously and becomes anxiously immersed in detail, how can he possibly throw off the temptations of the external world and maintain the stability and unaffected detachment of his inner being? If he masters an attitude of "Neither joy in the material nor sorrow in self" (remaining unaffected by the good or bad of the external material world or by personal ups and downs), then he will gain an attitude of mind that is both calm and composed, that in affairs enables him to advance and retreat at will, that allows a measure of expansion and that is stable and well-founded and yet active and unrestrained.

107. *Heaven and earth last for eternity but our bodies only this once; man may live a hundred years and the days slip easily by. Living in joy we cannot but know the happiness of life but we should also be aware of the sorrow of a life wasted away.*

Compared with eternity, man's life passes in haste, how can that not cause us regret? In determining how we should seize this transient life, which life skills can be reckoned as other than a waste of time? Treasure the time that there is, live in the moment, go forward positively and contribute to society, only then can the life of man resemble a drop of water that is absorbed by the sea and never dries up.

108. Resentment is displayed through virtue, thus it is better to ignore both resentment and virtue rather than expect people to behave virtuously towards one; hatred is established through benevolence, thus it is better to sweep away both hatred and benevolence rather than expect people to know one's benevolence.

Love and hate, kindness and complaint are closely connected, although mutual distinctions exist between them. How could there be the depth of hatred and grievance in parting unless there had been a similar depth and sincerity of love in the first place? If people are not always thinking of your affection and virtue, how is it that in times of disappointment, resentment is naturally added to dissatisfaction of heart? Do not demand of others that they should be benevolent and virtuous but demand of yourself that you should be without resentment or animosity.

109. The ills of old age are the fruits of youth; the disasters of one's decline are the consequences of one's success. Thus it is that the gentleman at the height of his powers must exercise extreme caution.

It is often said that: "In satisfaction never forget disappointment, in achieving power never forget the possibility of losing it." Leaving aside normal fluctuations in fortune, one should perform more good works and accumulate hidden merit at the height of success in order to avoid leaving a legacy of evil deeds that will entangle you in lawsuits when you fall from power. On top today but at the beck and call of others tomorrow; with money in your pocket today but adrift on the streets tomorrow. In times of peace one should think of danger and leave oneself a way out.

110. It is better to win over public opinion than to seek to buy hearts and minds; it is better to deepen old friendships than to seek new acquaintances; it is better to plant the seeds of hidden virtue than to seek fame and honor; it is better to stick to the ordinary than worship the extraordinary.

There are people in society today who, in a feat of image engineering, like to make a great display. They achieve some minor success and blazon the news abroad, their only fear being that people may not know. Their help for others derives mainly from selfish considerations. It is because of this that, however great their achievements, they can never really win people's hearts. A gentleman will never waste time and effort on self-promotion but will genuinely take practical steps to help all.

111. The principles of justice must not be violated, such violation will bring shame for generations; the secret ways to power and influence should not be taken, once taken there will be a stain for life.

A man should hold to the fundamentals as he faces the world. The fundamentals of society are social fairness and individual justice. If these are openly trampled upon this will inevitably arouse the condemnation of public opinion and the contempt of later generations. Those who take risks for their own advantage will find it difficult to escape the punishment of the law and the judgment of morality; for the man of moral integrity there are things that he will do and things that he will not do. Bribery and fraud and flattery for favors may bring a moment of glory but will bring ruin for a generation.

112. It is better to incur hatred through upright conduct than to gain favor through perverting one's principles; it is better to suffer slander through virtuous behavior than to win praise through wickedness.

Magnanimity and an upright manner are the most important qualities in the pursuit of wealth and happiness in life. Those who do ill to themselves in order to pander to others, or those who appropriate the reputation of others for their own prestige will be exposed in the end and will earn the contempt of all. The record of the sayings of Confucius and his disciples—*Analects* describes the gentleman as openhearted and well-grounded and the rogue as haggling over every penny and obsessed with profit and loss. A gentleman who enjoys the respect of others is able to preserve his goodness of heart and maintain independence of mind. Even though his upright character and straightforward conduct may attract the hatred of the rogue, his confidence will remain unshaken.

113. In family disputes one should be relaxed rather than intense; in dealing with the deficiencies of friends one should admonish sincerely rather than acquiesce.

The family is the place where the ties of affection between relations are created and love is the best means of dissolving contradictions. When contradictions appear within the immediate family one should advise and encourage with emollient speech, throw the light of reason on the problem and persuade with affection. Fierce abuse and decisions based on emotion will only exacerbate the contradictions and make things worse; with friends one should enjoy mutual respect but when they have done wrong one should not acquiesce indulgently or turn a blind eye. Despite the possibility of temporary misunderstanding, be straightforward in advice in order to avoid any further slide towards the abyss of error.

114. The true hero is punctilious in little things and does not exploit darkness to perform shameful acts, nor does he give up in despair when the road ahead becomes difficult.

The true hero can see things from a broad perspective but he can also manage the detail, standing tall before all and remaining disciplined when out of sight, mighty in success but honed by adversity. It is only this heroic type that will possess the courage and mastery of stratagem, the flexibility and the heroism both within and without. For the rest, the bold bandits of the wild, outwardly impressive, are beneath contempt.

115. It is difficult to buy the friendship of an hour with a thousand pieces of gold but a single bowl of rice will earn the gratitude of a lifetime. Thus it is that deep love may turn to hatred but indifference may breed happiness.

The feelings between people are extremely subtle. The proverb has it that "A single bowl of rice may bring a benefactor but ten bowls earn an enemy." The Han dynasty (206 BC–AD 220) general Han Xin (?–196 BC), in straitened circumstances in his youth, was once given a bowl of rice by an old woman washing clothes on the banks of a river. He never forgot this and later repaid her charity with a thousand pieces of gold. Conversely, if in helping others one just considers nothing but giving generously it may merely encourage idleness on the part of the recipient, so that when, one day, the charity diminishes, the recipient is not only ungrateful but may even turn to hatred, hence "ten bowls earn an enemy." This is due to a common character fault: once accustomed to receiving one soon forgets gratitude.

116. Conceal cleverness beneath stupidity, be reticent rather than obvious, harbor purity within the turbid, be cautious rather than foolhardy, these are the ways to face the world and the hidden burrows in which to retreat.

The *Daodejing* says: "Great wisdom may appear as stupidity and agility as clumsiness." Truly wise men may normally appear utterly stupid and seem as if chaotic and hesitant, they will not display knowledge or skill, or scheme shrewdly, or pretend to nobility and virtue, or toady for favor and gain. In Chinese philosophy this is the realm of the person of elevated character who conducts himself with wisdom. The personal cultivation and skills that do not advertise the abilities properly concealed by modesty, that allow other people space and that conceal talents beneath a bushel, these are the hidden burrows in which one may safely hide oneself. They will enable you to cope calmly with any difficulty and overcome any crisis.

117. *The scenery of failure and decline is to be found in the land of success, the seeds of opportunity are to be found scattered in decay. Thus, the gentleman dwelling in peace and order should have a care for misfortune, and in the midst of change should be resolute and long-suffering in order to achieve success.*

The *Book of Changes* says: "The sun past its zenith declines and the moon once full wanes." This cycle of rise and fall is a universal law that applies to heaven and earth and all living things, our life itself is the same. The gentleman at his most successful may be situated in safety but must give thought to danger and maintain a coolheaded vigilance; he should not feel discouraged in times of difficulty but, in a spirit of optimism, should resolutely and tenaciously strive to overcome them.

118. Those with a taste for the strange and novel lack deep knowledge or broad vision; those who strive excessively to preserve their moral integrity on their own cannot maintain it forever.

In this great cosmos, amongst the myriad manifestations of nature and every sentient being, each and every individual is different. There are those who take pleasure in the unconventional and those who prefer the simple and ordinary. In terms of Chinese philosophy, the propagation of individuality, whilst doubtless a good thing, requires a grasp of proportion: overdone it can lead to serious problems. Those who hold a blind belief in the unconventional and live isolated from the mass of people may outwardly appear to have individuality and to earn praise for it but have a difficulty with hard work and effort and keeping their feet on the ground. The true practice of self-cultivation requires us to return to the red dust of the mundane world and to come down to earth.

*119. Amidst the flames of anger and the torrents
of desire, one knows both the error of them and
the difficulty of controlling them. Who is it that
understands this and who is it that committed it? In
such a predicament, to be able to suddenly wrest one's
thoughts away will turn evil to truth.*

Buddhism holds that the birth of a virtuous thought will
bring a sense of the Buddha to all sentient beings; the birth
of an evil thought will bring an evil mind to all. Becoming
a Buddha or a demon is the matter of a moment. Self-
cultivation means putting effort into the management
of one's thinking, so that the Buddha mind comes to the
fore and the evil mind is extinguished. In the midst of
the raging furnace of anger and the boiling torrents of
physical desire, to know absolutely that it is wrong but
to stubbornly hold that it is uncontrollable, is a form of
temptation in itself. It is the evil mind that commands the
deed and the Buddha mind that brings the realization that
it is wrong. By gritting one's teeth, digging in one's heels
and banishing evil thoughts, one may transform the evil
mind even as it performs wickedness, into the Buddha
mind with knowledge of error.

120. Do not be deceived through believing a one-sided account, do not give way to caprice through a sense of one's own correctness; do not use one's own abilities to denigrate the lack of them in others, do not envy the talent of others because of one's own stupidity.

Listen to both sides to achieve understanding, believe only one for mystification. Mistaken judgment often arises from just listening to one side of a story. It is only by listening to a variety of opinions that one can make the right decision and not be led blindly into error by the evilly intentioned. The enlightened Tang dynasty Emperor Taizong (599–649), extended the boundaries of discourse between throne and officials and was open to advice, seeking it on a number of occasions from his straight-speaking chancellor, Wei Zheng (580–643), and ushering in the Zhenguan era of good government. However, there were emperors who were misled by the flattery of treacherous ministers, like the second Qin emperor (230–207 BC) who believed his minister Zhao Gao (?–207 BC), thus leading to murder and assassination and the collapse of the dynasty within two generations. The aspect of self-cultivation most closely linked to the concept of understanding through listening impartially is the practice of modesty and the capacity to receive and accept in order to achieve. A man needs vitality, drive and heroism, but not selfish willfulness.

*121. The shortcomings of others should be repaired
with tact. To expose and display them is to attack one
shortcoming with another; obstinacy should be handled
with delicacy, anger and hatred merely strengthen
obstinacy with obstinacy.*

Proper conduct in society is an art. Dealing with people's
mistakes and defects requires an additional degree of
tolerance and generosity, this is the only correct way
of helping to educate people and the only correct way
of achieving a good outcome. When confronted with
an obstinate person one should consider how receptive
they are, one should take into account their feelings and
their self-respect and guide them gently and patiently to
an understanding. Do not rush fanatically straight to the
point, even less should you seek an eye for an eye and a
tooth for a tooth by criticizing them fiercely, otherwise
the result will be the opposite of what you intended. Leave
people a little room and there will be space for you too.
Giving is one of the joys of life, tolerance is a quality of
happiness. Haggling over every detail, seeking revenge
for the slightest offence and making a mess of personal
relationships will cause setbacks at every turn.

122. Do not open your heart to the pitiless man of few words; guard your speech with the stubbornly indignant.

The proverb has it: "Do away with the malicious heart, do not dispense with the vigilant heart." To operate in the world one has to be skilled in the judgment of speech and the detection of expression, to know people and to distinguish one kind from another. When you encounter people whose expression is dark and foreboding and who speak little, do not put all your confidence in them. When you meet people who are filled with conceit and self-righteousness do not speak carelessly. Disaster emerges from the mouth; avoid deep conversation in a shallow acquaintanceship. The only way to achieve one's true self and individuality in society is by prudence of speech and behavior and calm conduct.

123. When thoughts are confused, raise your guard; when thoughts are tense, lower your guard. Otherwise you will merely exchange the ills of confusion for the disturbance of anxiety.

The saying has it that: "The way of Wen and Wu was now tense now relaxed." Leniency and severity are mutually linked, the method by which kings Wen and Wu ruled the nation. Today it is a metaphor for the reasonable tension and relaxation of life and labor and ease in the workplace. Further, "Water once full will spill, strings once taut will break." Consequently, there must be a sense of proportion in every undertaking. The rhythm of life in society today is fast and the pressure of work heavy. We should learn how to achieve an appropriate level of leisure amongst the busyness of work. The blind pursuit of desire and the consequent physical overdraft make it very difficult to maintain a robust body and mind.

124. Clear blue skies turn to sudden thunder and lightning; gales and rain swiftly turn to fine weather. Can the workings of nature be stilled for a moment? Can the great void of the heavens be confined for an instant? Man, both body and soul, is like this too.

The clear skies of heaven are boundless but black clouds billow as well; there is sunshine and gentle wind but thunder and lightning at the same time. Nevertheless, no matter what it contains, the sky is always the same sky and does not change in the slightest. The heart of man is much the same; there is happiness and anger, grief and joy. There is light and dark and growth and decay; there is the rapid rise to success and disappointment and frustration. But no matter what the circumstances, man's original mind remains the same original mind, untrammeled and unencumbered, detached and at ease, pure and undefiled, simple yet lofty.

125. It is said that in overcoming selfishness and desire, if the recognition of it is too late then the will to overcome is not easy to exert. It is also said that if recognition only occurs when it is unendurable it is not easy to resist. Thus, recognition is a bright pearl that illuminates evil and will is the sword of wisdom that will behead it. Both are essential.

The greed, anger, and stupidity in men's hearts are the greatest obstacles to self-cultivation. They are the demons of temptation in the hearts of men and should be eradicated in two ways. First, by raising awareness, using pure wisdom to see through illusion; second, by sharpening the will and using that strong will to defeat selfishness and desire. It is only through the unity of action and awareness, where recognition and practice are sufficiently in place, that one can subdue the mind and gain enlightenment.

126. Recognition of deception by others should not be revealed in one's speech, consciousness of insult should not show in one's expression. There is an exhaustible meaning to this and limitless benefit as well.

It is obvious that in life, when one discovers that one has been deceived, the wisest way of dealing with it is to seek the right opportunity to seize the initiative without any change in speech or expression, rather than to fly into a thunderous rage of condemnation and revenge. Do not be quick to strike back when deceived, bearing the wrong for a while will enable you to see the situation more clearly and to take control of it.

127. Difficulty, adversity and poverty are the hammer and anvil upon which heroes are forged. Accept this tempering and body and soul will profit, accept it not and both will be damaged.

Circumstances make heroes and chaos produces outstanding men. The greatest significance of suffering in life is that it tempers the will. Stone is quarried from the deepest mountains and must undergo a myriad of blows of hammer and chisel. When faced with the storms and tempests of life, do not abandon ambitious ideals or tenacity of will but accept the baptism of fate and you will be able to raise yourself to stand with head in heaven and feet on earth.

128. Our bodies are like a little heaven and earth where joy and anger cause no offence and good and bad have bounds, that is the art of harmony; heaven and earth are like a great mother and father who cause people to be without hatred and matter itself without evil humors, this is the scene of peace and harmony.

Traditional Chinese culture emphasizes: "Man and heaven are as one," the unity of the mind of man with heaven and earth. The basis of "the Way of heaven" is respect for nature and living in harmony. The creator, supported by the strength of the harmonies of *yin* and *yang* and all sentient beings, nurtures everything that lives. If storms and tempests occurred all and every day, our colorful world would not exist; the heart of man is the same, if our faces were contorted with misery every day and we were always temperamental and moody, then there would be no color to life.

129. "Do away with the malicious heart, do not dispense with the vigilant heart." This is a warning to the unwary. "It is better to be deceived than to reveal the deception." This is a warning to the over-suspicious. Both warnings stand together, shrewd yet unsophisticated.

On the one hand, malice should be done away with because in harming others one inevitably harms oneself. But wariness is indispensable because of the need to increase one's vigilance and be clear-eyed so as to be able to detect the rogues and put disaster at a distance. On the other hand, one should not, as it were, starve for fear of choking or become over-cautious, seeing enemies under every bush because of anxiety over the activities of rogues. This will not only make you mean and suspicious but will cause you mental torment.

130. Do not obscure one's own vision on account of the suspicions of the crowd, do not ignore the advice of others because of one's own prejudices, do not damage the whole for the sake of petty advantage, do not exploit public opinion to advance one's own interests.

If you are convinced that your own views are correct beyond the possibility of error, then you should pay no attention to the doubts of the majority. You should not abandon your own ideas because everybody else is dubious about you. You need your own independent judgment to be able to lightly accept outside interference; yet at the same time, one must conduct oneself dialectically and not refuse to accept any other views because of the firmly held nature of one's own. One also needs to be farsighted in dealing with people and affairs and not damage the whole because of greed for trifling advantage or to satisfy personal selfishness under the cover of public discussion. Otherwise, although it may appear that you have gained some advantage, in the end you have harmed yourself.

131. Be not too swift to achieve intimacy with men of virtue, or to sing their praises before the event for fear of the slander of others; do not carelessly rid oneself of an evil companion or alert him beforehand for fear of revenge by false accusation.

It is often said that: "Relations with a gentleman are as mild as water, relations with a rogue are as thick as honey." Relationships with people of virtue are built on a normal association that cannot be pursued intentionally. The frantic pursuit of friendship may cause others to feel that you have an ulterior motive. If you no longer intend to continue a relationship with an ill-intentioned person, you should slowly distance yourself from him, cooling off so that he does not obviously sense your change of attitude. Thus, in establishing relationships with others you should consider the means and in terminating them you should consider the technique as well.

132. Conduct and repute as clear as the sun in a blue sky grow from darkened chambers and leaky rooms; strategies of state that can change the fate of nations spring from a glimpse of the abyss and the dangers of thin ice.

There is a Zen poem that says:

> "Without the cold that cuts the bone,
> No scent from the blossoming plum
> Ever greets the nostrils."

That is to say that one's spiritual character is tempered by a treacherous environment and one's achievements are wrested from the tortuous turmoil of the affairs of the world. The earliest Chinese collection of poetry, the *Classic of Poetry*, says:

> "Shaking with fear,
> On the brink of an abyss,
> Like treading on ice."

Meaning that one should be as careful as if confronted by an abyss or treading on thin ice. A prudent approach to the affairs of the world is the style of a gentleman. Faced by the dangers and difficulties of the world, one's dreams and achievements can only be realized through prudent initiative and effort.

133. Fathers are compassionate and sons filial, elder brothers are friendly and younger brothers respectful. Even carried to the utmost it should be thus and without the least thought of gratitude. If the benefactor assumes he is granting a favor and that the recipient should show gratitude, then these become the manners of strangers and the ways of the market.

The family is the home of love and affection and not a trading place, nevertheless, many families harbor misconceptions on this point. Parents demand that their children should act according to their plans without considering whether these arrangements are acceptable or not; thus, children reciprocate the grace bestowed upon them through being raised by their parents with money. The compassion of parents and the mutual friendship and respect between brothers derive from the nature of mankind. If the affection that exists within the family gives rise to the idea of grateful recompense then that is equivalent to turning flesh and blood emotions into a market transaction.

134. If there is beauty then it must be matched by ugliness, if I do not proclaim my beauty then who may call me ugly? If there is purity then it must be opposed by filth, if I do not flaunt my purity who may call me filthy?

Daoism lays stress upon a dialectical method of thinking, believing that "have and have not, with and without are born of each other, difficult and easy are a whole." All contradictions exist in a state of mutual correspondence. So that without beauty there can be no ugliness; without cleanness there can be no dirt. Buddhism takes it a step further and points out that the source of the concept of differences between the myriads of things lies in the sense of distinction in the human mind. In life our speech and conduct attract all kinds of criticism, there is approval and opposition and praise and vilification. This requires Buddhist wisdom, neither to have one's head turned by the chorus of admiration nor to hang one's head in despair at the slander. Navigating the storms of life, one should not be obsessed with the changing external world with a mind inhabited by a sense of distinction. One should determine one's own direction before one can set sail for distant shores.

*135. Flame and frigidity of mood are more pronounced
in the wealthy than the poor; envy of heart is fiercer
at home than abroad. Unless this is managed calmly
and controlled peacefully, there will rarely be a day
without distress or vexation.*

The Tang dynasty poet Bai Juyi (772–846) wrote:

"Pity the luckless life of the youthful beauty,

In the heartless palaces of emperors and kings."

All the historical palace struggles have been like this. In the
struggle for power and advantage at court there have never
been any scruples about the slaughter of close relatives, or
mutual hatred, jealousy, and suspicion. No matter whether
in the homes of the wealthy or of the ordinary, the ugly
situations caused by mutual competition between brothers
and amongst relatives are enough to make you sick. When
you experience these kinds of situations, where attitudes
range from the inflamed to the frigid, it will be impossible
to reconcile and resolve them unless they are managed
calmly and sensibly, otherwise all will collapse into a heap
of anxiety and vexation.

136. One should not be confused about the merits and defects of others, to be so will engender an attitude of degradation and despair; one should not show favor and criticism too clearly, to do so may lead to disloyalty and rebellion.

If you are not properly clear about somebody's merits and defects it then becomes very easy to confuse right and wrong and cause suspicion and complaint. For example, management can only fully mobilize the positivism of its employees if it has clarity about their strengths and weaknesses and praise and criticism are in proportion. A person's partiality for love or hate cannot be expressed too obviously. Someone whose feelings of love and hate, like and dislike, are clearly differentiated, may admittedly lack many slippery characteristics but he makes enemies easily and is of no use in uniting all possible strengths. In recruiting talent, management cannot be partial otherwise it would be unfair, and of no help in uniting staff.

137. The salaries of officials should not be excessively generous, a generous salary is a danger; ability and talents should not be exercised to their utmost lest they fail through exhaustion; one's morality should not be obviously superior lest it attract slander and disaster.

Fortune and disaster each depend upon the other; things taken to extremes must recoil. A day of glory and disaster looms. Most outstanding ministers in ancient China were assassinated, an important factor being that their rank and position were too high and they were unable to seize the opportunity to escape. For example, the three distinguished ministers of the early years of the Western Han dynasty, who supported Liu Bang (256 or 247–195 BC) in his conquests, all met very different fates: Xiao He (?–193 BC) incurred Liu Bang's suspicion in his later years and was imprisoned; Han Xin's complete family was murdered, including his father and mother and relatives on his wife's side; the only one of the three to make a good end was Zhang Liang (?–189 BC) who resigned and became a hermit. The fate of these three great ministers demonstrates that the higher the office the greater the danger. All reigns and dynasties were the same.

138. Abhor evil done by stealth, abhor good done in the open. Thus, evil done in the open is no great disaster but evil done by stealth is a catastrophe; good done in the open is of little merit, while good done by stealth is merit indeed.

The wicked that openly indulge their wickedness are mere minor evildoers; evil deliberately concealed is the act of a major evildoer against whom one should take strict precautions. The minor evildoer is easily detected and dealt with, the major evildoer is more difficult. There must be a discount on the virtue of someone who does a little good and then proclaims it widely, raising suspicions about his motives. Good deeds performed in silence without any admixture of a desire for fame and profit are much more likely to attract respect and affection.

139. Virtue is the master of talent and talent the servant of virtue. To possess talent but not virtue is like a household without a master run by its servants, how can this not be a recipe for being overrun by goblins and demons?

The Northern Song dynasty political figure Sima Guang (1019–1086) said: "When virtue outstrips talent, that is a gentleman; where talent outstrips virtue, that is a rogue." In the traditional culture of China, morality has always been the most treasured quality. In any comparison between morality and talent, the man brimming with talent will always win in the short-term; however, in the long-term it is virtuous conduct that really determines the value of someone's achievements. There is a Chinese saying, "When morality is high, repute is vast." It is the man of talent who is equipped with a brilliant moral character who can really win over the hearts of men.

140. When digging out traitors and opportunists, they should be offered a way out. To give them no means of escape is like blocking rats in a hole, if all exits are blocked the good will be devoured by the bad.

The proverb says: "The man in dire straits fights for his life, the dog in dire straits jumps over the wall." A man with no way out is capable of extremes of behavior. The evildoer should be given an opportunity to reform and renew himself. Slaughter to the last man will arouse a frenzied counter-strike and will damage both sides equally and leave nobody the winner.

*141. One may share the blame with another but
not the glory, for equal glory leads to mutual
recrimination; one may share hardship with another
but not ease, for shared ease leads to hatred.*

The heart of man is unpredictable and desire is never
satisfied. It is easy to achieve unity in shared hardship
and in the face of storm and tempest to overcome
difficulties together. When it comes to assessing merit and
bestowing reward, people vie with one another to the
point of suspicion, jealousy and enmity. The ancients said:
"Once the birds are shot, hang up your bow." Historically
speaking, the majority of the great ministers who suffered
hardship in helping their monarchs in their successful
conquests were the victims of jealousy and came to no
good end. The wise man should be sufficiently aware of
people's character weaknesses and thus take a cooler view
of individual achievement. There will only be space for
yourself in this world of ever-shifting relationships if you
cease to strive after fame and fortune.

142. By reason of poverty, a gentleman may not be able to help others materially but when he encounters someone mired in obstinacy a mere word may warn him; when he meets someone in difficulty and saves him with a word, that is virtue beyond measure.

The well-educated intellectual, when he comes across someone in difficulties, may not be able to offer material assistance. Nevertheless, even if he cannot, a kind word is an act of virtue. For example, when someone feels that they have been wronged, put in a good word for them. Warn them when they are in danger and encourage them when they are dispirited. Help to others is not necessarily measured in terms of money. The seeds of compassion may be sown spiritually and accumulate virtue.

143. To rely on others in times of need but to distance oneself when things are going well, to fawn on the well-off but to abandon the impoverished, these are common failings.

It is a universal failing and weakness to be attracted to wealth and power. In times of desperate poverty one attaches oneself to anybody who will offer one a bowl of rice and then, when comfortable and well-fed, take off into the distance. The ancients said: "Nobody asks after you when you live in poverty in a busy town, distant relatives crowd to your door if you live in the hills in wealth." If you approach everything calmly and normally then you will not be troubled by the ups and downs of events and changes in relationships.

144. The gentleman is calm, cautious and detached; he does not forcefully speak his mind.

Endurance and tolerance are some of the better qualities in the art of handling life. Impetuosity can lead to disaster; patience may dissolve ill feeling. The wise man will always calmly assess the situation whatever the circumstances and will not stir up unnecessary trouble because of a moment's impetuosity or emotional judgment. The gentleman must maintain a degree of warmth and yet deal with events coolly and calmly. He must face the complications of the world with a smile and a relaxed attitude.

145. Virtue follows magnanimity and magnanimity grows from wisdom. Thus, to increase one's virtue one must extend one's magnanimity; and to extend one's magnanimity one must increase one's wisdom.

All of us, in society, exercise and display our individuality and the true colorfulness of society is only apparent when that individuality is sufficiently displayed. Nevertheless, it is precisely because of this display of individuality on the part of everyone that contradictions and clashes of personality are difficult to avoid. This is when depth of insight can increase patience and endurance and bring a little more acceptance, tolerance and understanding to different people and different circumstances. Then, an extension of magnanimity promotes an elevation of moral character that becomes the greatest bonus in your comparative superiority.

146. The lamp glows dimly and the sounds of the universe are stilled, this is when we sleep; we wake from dawn dreams and the world has yet to stir, this is when we emerge from chaos. Seize the moment to look back, reflect and know that hearing, sight, speech and smell are shackles that bind us and that lust and indulgence are the devices of loss and confusion.

As the evening sky darkens and all becomes still we drift peacefully into sleep and our minds regain tranquility. The sky brightens at dawn and the desires of our deep sleep begin to wake. This is the point at which we should tidy up our inner mind: are these swirling desires really the true features of our heart? Are the pleasures that delight eye and ear really the true joy of our soul? It is only when we can eliminate the deceptions of desire and abandon the superficial pleasures of the senses that we can truly achieve a higher level of sublimated wisdom.

147. Those capable of self-examination take everything as a warning, those that think ill of others come armed at every thought. One opens the road to virtue, the other deepens the springs of evil, the difference between heaven and earth.

The ancients said: "Sit in contemplation and consider one's own faults, converse lightly but do not discuss the faults of others." The Confucians emphasized the merits of self-examination and believed that in conduct and affairs one should look to the causes of difficulty in oneself and never blame events or other people. Confucius, the founder of Confucianism, said: "See worth and emulate it, see worthlessness and look into oneself." In this way, anything at all may form the steps to the promotion of self-progress. Conversely, to put the blame on others when encountering difficulties and to be concerned solely with condemning heaven and blaming men, then, each angry outburst is a step towards the brink of disaster.

148. Undertakings and achievements decay as the body decays but the spirit remains new forever; fame and riches change with the times but for righteousness and integrity a thousand years are as a single day. The gentleman does not exchange these spiritual ones for those physical others.

Zuo's Commentary on the Spring and Autumn Annals says that there are three kinds of enduring paths or ways: first the "establishment of virtue," next the "establishment of accomplishment" and then the "establishment of concept." The "establishment of accomplishment" refers to undertakings but these are great and enduring undertakings that may be passed on, self-seeking or selfish undertakings disappear without trace; the "establishment of concept" refers to writings but they are classic works rich in substance and form, not vacuous exercises in ornate language. No matter when or where, a man must "establish virtue" and maintain nobility of moral character and integrity. Achievement is for the moment, wealth and honor are not long-lasting but the spirit is immortal and moral integrity lasts forever.

149. A fishing net is for catching fish, but sometimes it so happens that a goose is trapped; a praying mantis is greedy for the cicada, unaware that a sparrow is poised behind it. Mysterious contrivance hides further mystery and change produces further change, what wisdom is there then that can be relied upon?

The proverb says: "The sandpiper struggles with the clam but the fisherman catches both," "the praying mantis catches the cicada but there is a sparrow behind." This is the way of the world, concealing within itself some sinister contrivance. People are often too clever by half with the result that they are hoisted by their own petard. If someone always intends to cheat others and harm them to his own advantage, the consequence will be the opposite and he will achieve his own destruction and will be spurned by all.

150. To conduct oneself without wholehearted sincerity is to become a mere ornament and without substance; to engage with the world but to lack liveliness of interest is to become a man of wood, beset by obstacles.

Nobility of behavior lies in sincerity of heart. Personal relationships should be based on mutual sincerity. The cunning rogue, even if he can prosper by deceit for a while, will not manage for a lifetime. A man should work and live in a style that is both warm and accommodating, and flexible. To be died-in-the-wool dogmatic is to be like a man of wood, seemingly stiff and stupid.

151. Without waves water is of itself calm, without obscurity a mirror is bright. Hence, there is no need to forcefully cleanse the heart, merely rid it of confusion and its clarity will shine forth; there is no need to strive after happiness, eradicate suffering and happiness will be there of itself.

Buddhism teaches us to "clarify the heart and see its nature," while Zen says "in the clear heart the water reflects the moon, when the consciousness is settled the sky is cloudless." The surface of the lake of the spirit is not disturbed by the breezes of desire and the bright moon of wisdom shines forth. The mirror of the soul is not obscured by dust so that the glory of human nature can blaze in splendor. As we live in the world, the existence of both desire and passion goes without saying but there must also be wisdom and reason. Just succumbing to desire and the satisfaction of one's personal interests rather resembles raising waves on the surface of a lake or obscuring a mirror with dust, all that is left of the original joy and happiness of life is endless vexation, suffering, and hatred.

152. The thoughts that touch upon the forbidden realm of ghosts and spirits, the words that harm the harmony of heaven and earth, the matters that spell disaster for children and grandchildren, these are to be prohibited most.

The red dust of the mundane world is the place of the practice of self-cultivation. Every thought, word and event in life is a whetstone upon which our moral character is honed and the place where the acquisition of virtue through self-cultivation starts. *Platform Sutra* says: "The enlightenment of man comes from the cleansing of the heart." The truly enlightened person must spend time on his thoughts and consciously eradicate evil ideas in order to overcome the character weaknesses of greed, anger and ignorance. Vicious practices that harm heaven and damage reason must be consciously controlled and kept at a distance.

153. Matters made unclear by haste may be clarified at leisure and impatience must be curbed for fear of provoking anger; give those who fail to accede to your direction a little space and they may change, never press them, it will only encourage stubbornness.

The *Analects* says: "The desire for haste prevents completion." When matters are at an impasse it does no harm to relax and back off for a while, thus allowing space to breath. To always be embroiled in a problem is of no help in solving it. It is the same when instructing others. When you encounter the stubborn and unreasonable, it does no harm to follow their line of thought as matters develop so as to lose no further opportunity of offering advice and retrieving the situation. Delighting in the sound of one's own voice and imposing one's own views will, on the contrary, produce an unsatisfactory result.

154. Even if one's conduct were of a cloud-like superiority to officials and the nobility, and even if one's writings had the perfection of driven snow, if they were not fired in the kiln of morality they would merely be a passing whim or a minor accomplishment.

Pottery must be fired before it can serve as a vessel, and iron ore must be smelted to make steel. Great talent and outstanding literary ability that lack a moral basis, that do not benefit all or serve the common good and are confined to a narrow selfish interest may appear elegant but are of no help to the world. They demonstrate a kind of virtue and learning that is both arrogant and insignificant, they resemble the utterly lifeless paper cut-out flowers. This is no example to follow.

155. One should withdraw from office at the height of one's powers, one should live in the world in second place to others.

Fireworks blaze in splendor but disappear at their most magnificent, giving rise to the well-known phrase, "eternity lies in a moment." The life of man is like this. When at the height of one's powers one should understand the principle of withdrawing when victorious. Do not wait until the sun sets behind the western hills before thinking of withdrawal. One should work in a spirit of selfless dedication just as the famous Northern Song dynasty minister Fan Zhongyan (989–1052) said: "First suffer the woes of the world, then rejoice in its joys." This requires a sense of responsibility rather than a headlong rush towards plunder for personal profit.

156. Exercise virtue in the very least of matters, bestow charity on those who cannot repay.

The cultivation of a virtuous character is like the saving of money, it has to be done drop by drop. Even in the smallest of things one should make rigorous demands upon oneself so as to build up good habits. Sometimes even a smile can light up the heart of another and illuminate the path of life so that splendor appears everywhere. In helping others, it goes without saying that one should aid those truly in need, even if they lack the ability to repay. Otherwise this help degenerates into a performance put on for one's own self-glorification; or a business transaction, in which greed for recompense only serves one's own self-interest.

157. It is better to befriend an old hermit in the hills than a town dweller; it is better to visit the humble homes of ordinary folk than call at the vermilion doors of the wealthy; it is better to listen to the songs of woodcutters and herdsmen than the gossip of streets and alleys; it is better to talk of the wise words and virtuous conduct of the ancients than discuss the excesses and shortcomings of people today.

What sort of friends should one make so that life may benefit? Only friendships built on the basis of morality, character, courage and sincerity will last and remain constant despite wealth and honor, greed, disaster and gain and loss. Someone who makes friends with a collection of lowlifes and listens to conversation that is mainly about speculation and the pursuit of profit will be easily infected by vulgarity. He would be far better off making friends with those who are simple and straightforward and have some refinement, who are unconnected with the powerful and who possess a balanced harmony and morality. The frequenting of the establishments of the rich and powerful may lend one the appearance of being a person of ability but all one hears is of the struggle for power, wealth and fame. This easily confuses the mind. It is better to make friends with ordinary people and observe life at its most real, with neither affectation nor hypocrisy; this is the way to achieve sincerity.

158. Virtue is the foundation of enterprise; no building has ever stood long upon insecure foundations.

A man without character, however able he may be, will find it difficult to go far. Which of the wicked men of history ever lacked ability or talent? Even though they may have enjoyed a moment of glory, in the end they and their families perished utterly, leaving a legacy of perpetual infamy. This is why a virtuous character is considered the basis of conduct. The conduct of an enterprise requires a basis of morality before it can develop and prosper in the long term.

159. Good character forms the root of succeeding generations; it has never been that branch and leaf flourish from roots that do not grow.

The *Book of Changes* says: "Those that accumulate virtue will have joy and more; those that accumulate evil will have disaster and more." A virtuous and benevolent character brings good luck with it. People who practice benevolence and accumulate virtue, who are of good character and who are enthusiastic in helping others, will gain the intimacy of neighbors and friends and will bring down blessings upon children, grandchildren and succeeding generations. Unscrupulous evildoers will bring destruction upon their own heads and suffering upon their descendants.

160. Our forbears said: "Abandoning the inexhaustible treasure of one's own family is to take up an alms bowl and beg from door to door." Also: "The suddenly rich should not boast of their wealth, for who is there whose stove fire lacks this smoke?" One is a warning to those who cannot perceive what they already possess and the other a warning to those who boast of their possessions. Both are behaviors that should be strenuously avoided by the learned.

Buddhists tell us that we can all become a Buddha. All sentient beings are equal and each of us possesses the sense of enlightenment that enables us to become a Buddha. This sense of enlightenment is our original mind and true character, an inexhaustible and eternal treasure. We remain stubbornly ignorant of how precious this treasure is and insist upon behaving like beggars, going from door to door with battered bowls. Why is it that people who have so much to start with turn themselves into beggars? It is because they do not stand by their original mind but are in pursuit of the outer world. If they looked back from their pursuit of the glamor of the external world and fixed their gaze upon their original mind, they could summon up the ability to live a different life. Nevertheless, if you are a person of consequence you should never indulge in arrogant boasting, the person of integrity must comprehend the principles of modesty and self-effacement.

161. The Way is a public matter that leads us according to our basic nature; learning is an ordinary meal that requires us to be vigilant at every turn.

The Way of heaven reaches its destination by different routes. In actual life, everyone's experience, basic nature, their comprehension of the way, their practice and the route they take are all different. Consequently, in teaching and transmitting the Way there must be a sufficient consideration of particular individual circumstances that differentiates between people and instructs according to ability. Scholarship is the same. One should be vigilant about every matter and not allow a single detail to obscure the whole. It is only thus, whether in the transmission of the way or in scholarship, that one may reap benefit in the end.

162. Others may not be wholly honest but to believe in them is to be honest oneself; others may not be utterly dishonest but to suspect them is to be dishonest oneself.

A gentleman is straightforward and openhearted, is candid in his dealings and does not suspect others without reason. Even when deceived he will not lose composure and will remain sincere. With a rogue it is the opposite. He measures the stature of a gentleman with the mind of a rogue believing that others are like him, brimming with treachery and cunning. Consequently, he will exhaust every possibility to secure advantage over others. It is rare to find people in the world today who believe in others and they are to be treasured. The finest aspect of a man's character is the ability to help somebody to stand above the dust of the mundane world.

*163. The generous thought nurtures all things on earth
like the wind in spring, it brings life at a touch; the
mean thought is like the hard winter snow that kills all.*

When faced with the same circumstances and in the
same environment, differences in mind-set usually
produce a different psychological reaction that in turn
influences our behavior. Kindhearted and generous people
conduct themselves in a gentle manner and are generally
approachable. Consequently, they enjoy good personal
relationships and people are willing to be their friends.
They are like the spring wind that nurtures, moves and
brings joy to all things. However, dealing with the mean
and uncharitable who haggle over every trifle and who
only have eyes for themselves is like suffering the blast of
an icy wind in a snowstorm; it makes the heart tremble
with the experience of disaster. To understand this is to
have a life with more happiness and less disaster, where the
path of life becomes broader at every step.

164. The practice of benevolence may show no advantage but it grows invisibly like a melon in the grass; the performance of evil may display no harm but it is like spring snow in a courtyard that must melt in the end.

There is a saying: "Virtue is the source of happiness." The tallest building grows from level ground and any achievement is built up bit by bit. It is the same with the practice of benevolence and the accumulation of virtue. One should not be relaxed because the harm of something appears trifling; it will grow day by day and month upon month and will develop into a major error. Nor should one disdain a minor act of charity; did any builder of a great enterprise ever fail to achieve bit by bit from small beginnings?

165. Old friendships should be treated with fresh enthusiasm; in hidden matters one's motives should be apparent; in dealing with the old and decrepit one's grace and manners should be outstanding.

The older the vintage the finer the wine. The more long-lasting the friendship the deeper the affection. Visiting friends should be warmly greeted and treated with sincerity. Empathize with the elderly who find it difficult to get around and treat them with respect. Help others today for you never know when you may be in difficulty yourself and need the help of others. If, in your conduct, you value sincerity and respect for others, then that is also a form of self-respect upon which you can create a more relaxed environment for personal relationships.

166. The industry of the diligent is devoted to the acquisition of virtue, but some people use it to relieve their hardship; the thrifty have little interest in money and profit, but some people use false thrift to conceal their meanness. In gentlemen it is a sign of virtuous conduct, in the hands of rogues it is a tool for selfish profit. Oh, what a pity!

The two great virtues of diligence and thrift have different objectives in the hands of gentlemen and of rogues. The gentleman uses diligence in the practice of self-cultivation; the rogue uses it in the pursuit of profit. The gentleman is plain by nature and is content with the simple life; the rogue uses the simple life as a pose to conceal his meanness. The gentleman's principles of conduct often become the tools of the rogue in his pursuit of advantage. For example, the peaceful use of nuclear energy produces electricity and heat to the benefit of mankind; there would be no greater tragedy for mankind than its use as a deadly weapon. It can be seen that the user determines the objective consequences. Thus, as we live in this world, we must clear our eyes and see with clarity who are the gentlemen and who are the rogues.

*167. When the enthusiasm of the moment expires,
its action dies with it; how is this not a step back?
Understanding achieved through emotion brings
bewilderment as well as comprehension; it is not a
lamp that shines forever.*

Buddhism regards wisdom as a "lamp that shines forever,"
and in no way an achievement gained through the
transmutation of the Seven Emotions and Six Desires that
derive from the sensory organs. Buddhism also likens the
transmission of wisdom to the "ever-turning wheel of the
law" that propagates the truth generation after generation,
relying not upon the enthusiasm of the moment but upon
a staunch belief and a constant resolve. Thus, to achieve
anything in life one must determine the right direction to
follow and control one's moods and emotions with reason,
separating what should be done from what should not be
done and forging ahead with untiring resolve.

168. One should forgive the sins of others but not one's own; one should endure the hardships and humiliation heaped upon oneself but ease those endured by others.

China has always emphasized the gentleman's belief that one should be "magnanimous towards others but severe with oneself." The gentleman of cultivation can only make good progress if he makes severe demands on himself and can only create good relationships if he treats others leniently and generously. If he faces his own difficulties resolutely, he will be strengthened in spirit, and compassion will flourish if he offers a helping hand when he sees others in difficulty.

169. To be able to divest oneself of vulgarity is unusual, but deliberately seeking to be unusual is not unusual at all but monstrous. It is pure to eschew filth but to advertise one's purity by ostentatiously abandoning vulgarity has nothing to do with purity and everything to do with seeking to be different.

It naturally requires a particular strength of character to be able to abandon the habits of the mundane world and to earn the admiration of its inhabitants. However, those who deliberately set out to make an exhibition of their difference from the common herd through various kinds of unconventional behavior or apparel are merely pretentious and little short of a disgrace. There are more than a few people in our society who flaunt their unconventionality or behave shockingly as a means of focusing attention upon themselves and take no account of the view that society or people generally may have of them. Doing an ordinary job, as long as one can persevere and keep at it over the years, that is no ordinary matter!

170. Charity should be bestowed frugally at first and generously later; be generous first and frugal later and people will forget your benevolence. Power should be exercised severely at first and leniently later; be lenient first and severe later and people will complain of your ruthlessness.

It becomes difficult to swallow if you eat the delicacies first and the coarse food later; do it the other way round and you will feel that you have dined well. This principle should apply to both management and personal relations. It is often said that "Power and Charity come together" or "Severity and Leniency are employed as one," in fact the ideal way of treating people is through a policy of "Severity first and Leniency later." Consequently, charity should be bestowed frugally first and generously later to prevent its acceptance becoming a habit and leading to unrealistic expectations; in establishing power severity comes first and leniency later, a gradual relaxation may follow.

171. If the mind is void the original nature shows; seeking to see the original nature with an unquiet mind is like looking for the moon in choppy water. If thoughts are clean the mind is pure; to seek clarity of mind without eradicating impurity of thought is like trying to see oneself in a dusty mirror.

If the pool of the mind is crystal clear the bright moon of wisdom will be reflected in it. If thoughts are clean it is like a clear cloudless sky that stretches on forever. The eminent Tang dynasty Zen Master Shenxiu (c. 606–706) said:

> "The body is a bodhi tree
> And the spirit a bright mirror and its stand,
> To be polished and swept
> Clean of the dust of the world."

Zen practitioners advocate "seeing one's nature through clarity of mind," likening the human spirit to a mirror. It is only by overcoming the multitude of distractions and maintaining purity of thought that one can, in deep tranquility, comprehend the wonders of life in the universe. Any practice not rooted in this principle, however devout it may be, is a waste of time.

172. All esteem me for my position, but it is just respect for crown and sash; all insult me for my poverty, but it is just contempt for sackcloth and sandals. In that case, it was not respect for me, why therefore should I rejoice? Nor was it contempt for me, why therefore should I be angered?

In all truth, one should be above the warm and chill and hot and cold of personal relationships. When you are flying high, it is your wealth and position that people respect and not necessarily you yourself, hence one should not be disproportionately self-satisfied when you are the object of flattery. In the same way, when you are dejected and poverty-stricken and are ignored and humiliated it is because you have neither power nor position not because of you yourself. We all enter this world of dust naked and empty-handed. If we can grasp this principle and maintain an ordinary state of mind, even in disappointment, we can remain as calm as ever.

173. The instruction of the ancients, "Leave food for the mice, douse lamps out of pity for the moth," is a means of prospering all life on earth. Without it we would just be soulless shells of mud and wood.

Chinese Buddhism calls upon us to embrace the concept of mercy and to treat others as we would treat ourselves. Every virtuous thought may be compared to a small star-like flame that gradually grows from few to many and acquires great strength. Hence, man must nurture charity and virtue to sow fields of happiness. In the exercise of charity and the accumulation of virtue one should not only consider oneself but should also take account of the weaker lives of the natural world. One should protect animals and leave them space to exist. Kindness to animals is also kindness to the very body of mankind itself.

174. The spirit of man is as the spirit of heaven: in joy like the propitious stars and auspicious clouds; in anger like earthquake and storm; in charity like gentle breezes and sweet dew; and in severity like the blazing sun or autumn frost. Which of these should we be without? As long as we accommodate ourselves to both rise and fall, no obstacle will stand in the way and we can become one with the great void.

The spiritual world of mankind is richly diverse in ideas that change from moment to moment. Man feels happiness, anger, sorrow and joy just as nature has wind, frost, rain, dew, darkness and light, gloom and brightness. The Daoists emphasize, "the Way is of and in the Natural World" believing that the uttermost realm of the practice of cultivation is to achieve unity with heaven. Although heaven contains all kinds of transient phenomena such as light and darkness, in itself it has never been subject to any kind of influence and remains vast, all-reaching and utterly without hindrance. Man, too, should be like this. Even though the Seven Emotions and Six Desires are always present and moods are unstable and rise and fall, the nature of wisdom is such that it can encompass everything, allowing these changes of mood but retaining the undisturbed tranquility and unimpeded spaciousness of the very essence of the mind.

175. *When unoccupied, the mind is easily confused, thus vigilance is necessary even when quiet; when busy, the mind is easily carried away, thus tranquility is required even when active.*

One who is unoccupied all day long becomes apathetic, his will is worn away and he enters a state of confusion and darkness. In this state one should remind oneself to maintain vigilance and rouse one's spirits. When one is active and rushing about all day, the mind is easily disturbed by trifles; it becomes over-taxed and can be carried away. In this state one should remind oneself to calm down and curb the urge towards uneasy impetuosity lest error comes of all this activity.

176. In the discussion of affairs one should stand apart but be aware of advantage and disadvantage; in the execution of affairs one should be involved but set aside the anxieties of advantage and disadvantage.

The saying has it: "The one involved is confused, the bystander is clear." There is a difference in feeling and point of view between involvement and non-involvement. Moreover, there is also a difference in the understanding acquired. Thus, in discussion one should adopt a fair and objective point of view as if standing on a summit and observing the course of events, before being able to comprehend the overall situation or discover the true nature of any problems. In the handling of affairs, it is only through personal involvement that one can acquire an adequate feel for the crux of a problem, the mastery of the detail and the ability to manage it.

177. *A gentleman who occupies a position of power should be firm in conduct but affable in disposition. He should not join corrupt cliques nor cause evil through excesses in behavior.*

The gentleman achieves excellence through learning and thus obtains office. For intellectuals, study followed by an official post is an important route into the world. Nevertheless, there is still a long way to go from study to an official post and from book learning to practice. Gentlemen have always been bookish by nature, full of ideals and over-discriminating in their handling of people and management of affairs. In fact, at the beginning of an official career, it is only possible to protect one's own interests through honesty and moral integrity. Otherwise, involvement with cliques and factions or taking decisions on the basis of emotion will lead to one's downfall and the loss of self. However, at the same time one must strive to learn the art of handling people and affairs, of being skilled in defending oneself, in mastering circumstance and in coordinating the strength of all sides for one's own use.

178. Those who make a display of virtuous conduct attract calumny thereby; those who exhibit their ethical learning often attract criticism thereby. Thus it is that the gentleman should neither come close to evil nor seek a reputation for virtue, for the true treasure of life is only gained by living in refined moderation and simplicity.

In China, there has always been an emphasis upon modesty and a low profile. A lack of pretension is desirable both in conduct and at work. Boasting of one's moral integrity and the breadth of one's learning may make one feel good but it makes it difficult to convince others and earn their respect. Moral repute and learning are not created by blowing one's own trumpet but are polished from hardship. Gentlemen of moral integrity would never use their moral repute and learning as capital to be invested in self-glorification. They are simple and modest, creating an extraordinary undertaking in the midst of ordinary circumstances.

179. When you encounter a cheat, move him with your sincerity; when you encounter a bully, warm him with your kindness; when you encounter a crook, encourage him with your virtue. In this way there will be none under heaven who may not be thus transformed.

In conducting himself in society the gentleman must not only master the art of dealing with people and affairs, there must also be a principled way of doing so. In dealing with rogues one must be able to make the most of it and gain what one wishes. This is because a gentleman possesses great virtue and is able to use it in the cultivation and subsequent transformation of others, in moving them and also in influencing them. Men are not trees or grass, who is there who lacks feeling? Even the craftiest of men has not entirely severed the roots of virtue. Treat the violent man with true feeling and he will become gentle and acquiescent; use moral conduct to encourage evildoers and their wickedness will disappear without trace. Convince others with virtue and the whole world will be both happy and receptive and of use to oneself.

180. A single benevolent thought may brew harmony between heaven and earth; a single drop of purity of heart will perfume a hundred generations.

A single benevolent thought and hell becomes heaven; one wicked thought and heaven turns to hell. As we live in the world it is only by having a heart of purity and virtue that we can enjoy the spirit of nobility and freedom. Love is the basic motive that allows mankind to multiply and prosper. When the merciful heart looks upon heaven and earth and all sentient beings, all is peace and happiness. Self-cultivation, morality and upright conduct will withstand the test of history, even for thousands of generations, and garner a glorious reputation.

181. Conspiracy and plots, strange practices and curious skills are the seeds of disaster within society. Only ordinary virtue and ordinary conduct can bring an end to primal chaos and usher in peace.

The Confucians preached the Middle Way, opposed the strange and novel, emphasized fairness and simplicity and stressed the need for gentleness and sincerity as well as plain honesty and dignity in behavior. The freakish, weird and peculiar gained no approval from the Confucians and were condemned for their irregularity of character. In Confucian eyes, the only truth lay in the plain and ordinary. Nevertheless, by no means did this mean that one should eschew all progress and innovation and lead a humdrum life without the need to do anything. Consequently, in today's society we should innovate boldly but be careful to maintain honesty and moderation on the road towards the search for change and novelty. We should carefully guard against the extremes of conduct and performance that lead to disaster.

182. The saying goes: "Endure the hillside track when climbing mountains, endure the dangerous bridge when walking in snow." The word "endure" has broad significance, as in dangerous situations or the rough passages in life where without endurance how could one avoid falling into a pit of thorns?

Emotions are like a rough sea and the paths of life twist and turn. In the course of life, one may encounter all kinds of difficulties. Zhuangzi said: "Those who show no fear in the face of great difficulties are heroes even amongst sages." When confronted with difficulty one must be confident in victory and have the courage to endure. The *Analects* said: "The scholar cannot be without resolve for his burden is great and the path is long." With perseverance and tenacity one can uproot the brambles and thorns, strive to achieve and eventually break through difficulties and obstructions.

183. Boasting of one's achievements and flaunting one's literary ability is to conduct oneself by relying on the external. One may be unaware of the treasures of one's own mind but if you retain its original nature, then you may still lead an upright life even though you have achieved little and written nothing.

The *Platform Sutra* says: "Enlightenment seeks only the mind within, why strive to seek for mysteries without?" The truth of happiness in life is to be found by returning and living within one's original mind. Any search outside is to pursue the material world out of a state of self-confusion or to arrive in a state of self-confusion through pursuit of the material world. Advertising oneself through the pursuit of achievement and literary display is to abandon the root for the detail. To seek Buddha outside one's own mind is not the path to true enlightenment. The truly enlightened person may not have a truly outstanding achievement or elegant piece of writing to his name but his spirit will still blossom in joy and flow with happiness.

*184. To steal leisure from activity one must first find
a purpose from within leisure; to find calm within
hubbub one must first establish a basis within calm.
Otherwise you will be at the mercy of changing
circumstances and the wear and tear of events.*

How does one seize leisure from activity or calm from
hubbub? Leisure and activity have to be combined and
calm and movement be in mutual correspondence. In
leisure prepare for activity and the mind will have some
means of control, so that when busy there is no confusion;
when calm one must establish a basis for coping with
hubbub so that the mind has the basic confidence to
remain undisturbed by the hubbub. To maintain one's
balance in a life of business and leisure, to maintain one's
stability in a life of hubbub and tranquility, that is the life
of true wisdom.

185. Do not betray one's own good nature, do not exhaust one's finer feelings or material strength, for these three may give heart to heaven and earth, life to the people and good fortune to one's descendants.

The scholar's ideal is to establish his moral virtue and conscience between heaven and earth, to define the meaning of life and create happiness for future generations. There are three ways of achieving this: first, by not betraying one's own conscience and being upright in conduct; second, through kindness and honesty rather than heartlessness and lack of feeling; and third, through contented frugality rather than excessive wastefulness. In this way, sublime ideals may be translated into practice.

186. There are two phrases that apply to the establishment of an official, "fairness brings justice" and "incorruptibility brings respect"; there also are two phrases that apply to a family, "mercy encourages calm and stability" and "frugality leads to sufficiency."

Because what is done above has an effect below, whether as an official or when running a household, one must set an example. To follow the path of an official one must be fair and selfless, incorruptible and self-disciplined. If officials cannot keep to the path of fairness and justice, the people will take advantage of the law to suit their own ends and disturb the stability of society. This is known as "if the rafters above are out of true the beams below will be crooked." Harmony is to be treasured in the running of a household, which should be maintained with careful frugality. The *Mirror for Government*, the historical chronicle in 294 parts compiled by Sima Guang of the Northern Song dynasty says: "Take in proportion, use with frugality and there will always be a sufficiency." There must be growth in the accumulation of family wealth but there must be economy as well. Long-term sufficiency can only be guaranteed by economy in household expenses and the avoidance of extravagance.

187. In wealth one must know the hardship of poverty; in youth and strength one must be aware of the misery of old age.

The life of man encompasses both moments of glory and of poverty and exhaustion; sometimes things go smoothly and sometimes not. When things are going well and at the height of one's glory, one should not be so satisfied as to wholly lose one's sense of proportion and become arrogant and self-satisfied. One should always be sensitive to the suffering of those in straitened circumstances. When you are young and healthy, you should not mock the weakness and disability of the elderly. Old age comes to us all in the end. "Lack of effort in youth brings sorrow in age." When we are young, we must lay the foundations of life so as to be able to cope effectively with the storms and tempests to come.

188. One should not be too perfect in behavior, one should be acquainted with humiliation and insult; one should not be too fastidious in dealing with people, one should tolerate all of virtue, evil, sagacity and stupidity.

Li Si (?–208 BC), the prime minister of the Qin dynasty (221–206 BC) said: "Mount Tai does not curb its fertile soil, hence its size; the sea and rivers do not abandon small streams hence their depth; monarchs do not repulse their people hence their virtue." The gentleman conducts himself with a large measure of tolerance. Everyone has their good and bad points. Confucius said: "When three walk together, one of them must be my teacher." In dealing with other people one must be skilled in discovering and learning from the merits of others before any real progress can be made. Observe the faults of others and swiftly seek out one's own, correcting them if they exist, if they do not then redouble your efforts.

189. It is not worth feuding with a rogue, he has his own enemies; it is not worth currying favor with a gentleman, he is not susceptible to flattery.

Birds eat insects and cats catch rats. That is the law through which nature maintains its balance. "Evildoers have their own axe to grind" and rogues their own enemies to fight. One should keep one's distance from ill-intentioned rogues and not waste one's efforts in meaningless disputes. In the same way, there is no need to fawn on a gentleman. The upright principles upon which a gentleman conducts himself in society will not allow him to bestow favors out of personal consideration or outside the law.

190. The ills of debauchery can be cured but the ills of obstinacy are difficult to cure; physical obstacles may be overcome but hindrances in reasoning are hard to set aside.

The Ming dynasty philosopher Wang Yangming (1472–1529) said: "Mountain robbers may be easily overcome but the robbers of the mind are hard to surmount." Getting rid of habits of thought, prejudice and other bad habits is harder than hard. The ills of debauchery can be corrected in the end through strict oversight; however, intellectual obstinacy, prejudice and ignorance will be beyond anybody's ability to cure unless they are corrected through an effort of self-examination. Consequently, one should first examine one's own thinking in all things to make sure that both thinking and point of view are correct before there is any possibility of making few errors.

191. Tempering self-discipline is like refining gold, nothing is achieved in a hurry; proper action is like drawing a hundred-pound bow, no great effect is achieved by drawing weakly.

Any profound and penetrating effort requires an iron bar to be ground down to a needle. There are no shortcuts in life. Everything requires steady effort. A desire for quick results will only end in superficiality. Only accumulation in depth will result in proper preparation. Opportunism and seeking a quick profit may secure a temporary advantage but it will be difficult to achieve anything long-lasting on such an insubstantial basis. If problems are considered with care and forethought, targets will be reached at the first try. Hovering over the water like a dragonfly will achieve nothing.

192. Rather be despised than flattered by a rogue;
rather be criticized than forgiven by a gentleman.

The sweet words and honeyed tones of the rogue are
never well-intentioned. Fine words that delight the ear
are a cause for vigilance and the maintenance of alertness.
A gentleman treats people with sincerity and even if
he criticizes you, it is out of loyalty. "One word from a
gentleman is worth a decade of book learning," one should
take the advice of a gentleman to heart. Otherwise, when
out of the goodness of his heart a gentleman forgives
you, you will have lost an opportunity for correcting and
improving oneself.

193. Those who seek profit step outside the bounds of morality and their harm is shallow but obvious; those who seek fame are concealed within the bounds of morality and their harm is hidden and deep.

It is often said: "Rather be a true rogue than a false gentleman." Those who openly seek fame and profit without concealing their liking for them, actually appear sincere and straightforward. Even if their behavior appears not to conform to morality, the harm is clear for all to see and easily prevented. It is the false gentleman who is most to be guarded against. Confucius said: "Fine words and a splendid appearance are seldom signs of virtue." These people conceal themselves amongst true gentlemen and exploit the goodwill of others for their own nefarious ends, their means are secretive and the damage they do is vast.

194. Failing to reciprocate the deepest favor but retaliating at the slightest grievance, believing the merest rumor of evil but disbelieving the obvious tidings of good, this is rancor carried to extremes and should be eradicated.

We should conduct ourselves in the world so that when we see outstanding people we learn from them but when we see evil people we should examine ourselves and strive to do better. Life is full of pitiless people who lack charity and who merely see the faults in others. They never reciprocate favors however great; they always seek the means to take revenge for any grievance. When they hear well of others they only half believe it; when they hear ill of others they believe every word. The gentleman should guard against this kind of selfish and cold indifference.

195. Slander and calumny are like a patch of cloud that obscures the sun but soon clears; fine words and flattery are like the silent draught that wrecks the body.

The proverb says: "Rumor ceases at the wise." Rumor and gossip are naturally harmful for a while but in the end, they are just that, rumor and gossip. Come the day when the water recedes and the rocks appear, the ugly visage of the rogue will be exposed. But the character of the gentleman who has been wronged will appear even more noble. The saying has it: "A gentle village is the tomb of heroes." Honeyed words are more to be feared than rumor and slander. One should always be vigilant in the face of them. The flattery of rogues may fall comfortably on the ear but in the midst of this comfort, vigilance may fail and one may gradually become arrogant and self-satisfied to the eventual destruction of self.

196. The summits of mountains are bare of trees but the winding valleys are rich with vegetation; river rapids lack fish yet deep pools and still water are full of them; this reflects the extremes of lofty behavior and excess of narrow attitudes that a gentleman should be scrupulous in avoiding.

The traditional culture of China has always advocated the Middle Way. The *Doctrine of the Mean* says: "Achieve balance and heaven and earth will be well positioned and all sentient beings will flourish." Heaven, earth and all beings flourish because of their richness and diversity. Whether in personal conduct or the management of affairs one should never go to extremes. Things taken to extremes will always rebound and difficult songs are seldom well sung, the gentleman must always be vigilant against this. In the handling of complicated situations and relationships one must master the norms of appropriate behavior and achieve a suitable balance.

197. Those who achieve are mostly balanced and well-rounded personalities; those who fail are inevitably stubborn and obstinate.

The traditions of Chinese culture have always valued harmony, promoted good nature in relationships and equability of method in affairs. In situations of rapid change there needs to be a flexible response before affairs can be brought to a successful conclusion. Sticking stubbornly to any kind of predetermined opinion or approach can only put obstacles in the way of change and development. Consequently, when problems occur, we should not be dogmatically inflexible but respond pragmatically on the basis of the reality of the situation. Even if it is impossible to achieve cooperation, one should not damage an atmosphere of harmony but should take a step back in the hope that an opportunity for cooperation may perhaps present itself in the future.

198. In one's conduct in society one should not be the same as the commonality of people nor yet different from them. In the handling of affairs, one should not inspire loathing nor yet cause ill-based joy.

Achieving a balance in one's conduct, inclining neither in one direction nor the other, is an art and more than an art, a form of self-cultivation. One does not wish to follow the surges of the sea and swim in a tide of dirt, nor does one want to set a fashion for indulging in the fragrance of one's own reputation; nor yet does one want to feel that one is inspiring loathing in other people or gaining their liking by ingratiating oneself. The skill of all this lies in careful thought. One can only achieve a command of appropriate behavior and balance through sufficient practice and experience.

199. As the sun sets so do the clouds shine with splendor; as the years draw to their close so are they bathed in the fragrance of oranges. Thus it is that at the end of the road the gentleman should redouble both effort and energy.

The ancients considered that during a lifetime there were three causes for grief: the fading of beauty, the decline of heroism and the exhaustion of talent. It is also said: "Sunsets are at their best only as the night approaches." As life approaches the evening of its later years, the glory has departed, senility approaches and the body is wracked with illness, a prospect of sadness difficult to avoid. At the same time, remorse and a sense of giving up can cause an earlier than necessary decline in vitality. The Wei dynasty (220–265) emperor Cao Cao (155–220) said in a poem:

> "The old steed lies in the stable,
>
> Its will departed ten thousand *li*.
>
> The warrior passes his declining years,
>
> His martial spirit still present."

But even in one's later years, man and nature are still as one and from the vigorous vitality that derives from the beauty of nature we can comprehend the reason for living and being. We must stimulate our enthusiasm for life and pass every day of life full of spirit.

200. The hawk stands as if asleep, the tiger crouches as if sick, tricks to deceive those whom they would devour. Hence, a gentleman should conceal his intelligence and obscure his talent before he can attain the strength of iron.

The hawk seems to be dozing but is incomparably alert; the tiger appears lethargic but is poised ready to spring. These are examples of their survival skills and areas of superiority. The Western Han dynasty historian Sima Qian, wrote in the *Records of the Grand Historian of China*: "The successful merchant conceals his wealth and appears empty-handed, the cultivated gentleman accumulates virtue but seems stupid." Shallow waters splash and burble, deep waters run still. In a society of toxic personal relationships, people with real strength conceal their abilities and do not lightly reveal their hand, so that when the occasion arises it comes like a bolt of lightning from a clear sky.

201. Economy is a virtue but in excess it becomes stinginess, a meanness that by contrast damages the elegance of one's style; modest reticence is a virtue but in excess it leads to obsequiousness, an obsession with the fine detail and an inclination to trickery.

People often say: "Too far is as bad as not far enough," truth in excess becomes falsehood. Thus, in conduct and in society one must always consider the question of "degree." Economy and modesty have always been the traditional virtues of the Chinese people but when there is an excess of economy and an unwillingness to spend on even the bare necessities of life, it raises the suspicion of stinginess, even of miserliness. This can cause people to lose the attitudes that should inspire one's behavior and lack interest in life. To be overly modest and to withdraw from everything can well cause people to suppose that there is some ulterior motive, so that an attempt to be clever turns instead to stupidity.

202. Do not worry over things that do not accord with your wishes, do not rejoice at pleasure, do not put one's faith in permanent ease, do not go in fear of initial difficulties.

Zen Buddhism tells us "the ordinary mind, that is the Way." Buddhism teaches us that we should face the complicated world calmly. If someone can maintain a calm and honest state of mind, they will naturally be able to resist the intrusions of the external world. Someone skilled in the Way should respond positively when confronted by unfavorable circumstances. The satisfaction of a moment is no cause for mad outbursts of joy. Joy is temporary and may turn to lasting harm and requires, rather, constant care. Permanent ease may turn stagnant and lack progress; it is only by ceaselessly pushing forward that one can realize the permanent ease of movement. Never recoil from difficulties; it becomes very difficult to succeed if, having failed at the first, one dare not take the second step.

203. Too much joy in feasting does not become the upright family, too much indulgence in pleasure does not become the true scholar, too much consideration of position and repute does not become the honest official.

Laozi said: "Rich colors blind the eye, beautiful sounds deafen the ear, delicate flavors confuse the palate, hunting at the gallop excites the mind, and unobtainable goods cause men harm." That is to say that rich colors cause the eye to lose the capacity for calm and clear sight, beautiful sounds rob the ear of the capacity to hear true sound, the variety and delicacy of flavors lead the palate astray, and the excitement of hunting sets one's pulse racing so that it is impossible to remain calm and coolheaded. Rare and valuable objects inspire covetousness, and cause hesitation and weakness of mind so that the practice of self-cultivation is brought to a halt. Living in luxury, the celebration of good times, status and salary, are all part of life's attachments that bring only the joy of a moment and where overattachment can lead to the loss of one's very self.

204. A man who considers the satisfaction of desire as happiness will be tempted into suffering thereby; the man of understanding regards the endurance of suffering as a joy and will in the end achieve happiness thereby.

The desires of man are inexhaustible. The moment one is satisfied another is born in a cycle of suffering brought about by unsatisfied desire. Caught up in this cycle, one's life loses its meaning. In fact, the happiness and joy of life lie in transcending material desire. The man who pans for gold endures all sorts of hardship in rinsing away the silt before he can obtain true gold. Man's success has always been achieved through the endurance of difficulties. Life's true path can only be reached through effort, by defeating difficulty and struggling for progress.

205. The full life resembles water in a pot filled to the brim, the addition of a single drop will cause it to overflow; the life lived dangerously resembles a tree about to fall, a single nudge and it will crash.

A single straw may be enough to break the back of a camel loaded to its limit. In life, there is always the final snowflake that snaps the tree branch and the final drop of water that breaches the dyke. Consequently, the gentleman of perception, in whatever situation, must always recognize the circumstances clearly. It is easy to be carried away by the unthinking enjoyment of bouquets and applause in times of success and glory. There is huge pressure upon the mind when beset on all sides by crisis and danger; the ability to free oneself of the world can help one escape melancholy.

206. A man must assess others with a cool eye, listen to speech with a cool ear, approach emotion with a cool heart and think with a cool head.

Daodejing says: "A hot temper may defeat the cold and tranquility defeat heat but calm will order all under heaven." In his *Admonitions to His Son*, Zhuge Liang (181–234) the famous minister of the period of the Three Kingdoms wrote: "In conduct a gentleman should be calm in the practice of self-cultivation and prudent in the growth of virtue." Cheng Hao (1032–1085) the scholar of the Rationalist School of the Northern Song dynasty said: "The calm appraisal of all living things brings contentment." A tranquil and honest frame of mind is the highest state for the cultivation of mind and body but even more it is the path to the attainment of wisdom. The cool assessment of others is the only way to avoid being deceived by appearances and to be able to see through to a person's true nature. Listen dispassionately and the heart will not burst with joy at sweet words and honeyed phrases or become distraught at unpleasantness. Correct judgment can only be arrived at through analysis conducted calmly and coolly. It is only by maintaining a clear mind and a cool head that it is possible to remain calm in the face of the multifarious events of life and grasp the initiative.

207. The man of compassion is openhearted and thus enjoys eternal good fortune and exists in a spirit of generosity; the mean-minded man is agitated in thought and thus sparse in fortune and reward and exists in a state of narrow-minded misery.

Buddhism teaches us: "To possess wisdom is to be without vexation; to possess mercy is to be without enemies." The life of a compassionate man is filled with warmth and love and brings comfort and harmony to the lives of others. Only a mind that is openhearted and generous can diminish selfish desires and vexation. By contrast, a person who believes himself clever, who employs cunning in all he does, and who regards everything in terms of advantage rather than morality, will always be defeated by his own cleverness and, even if he does secure a moment's success, will come to no good end in the long run.

208. When hearing of evil one should not rush to condemn for fear of giving vent to anger and malice; when hearing of virtue one should not immediately seek friendship for fear of attracting scoundrels to one's side.

"Listen to more than one view for clarity; listen to a single view for obscurity." It is only possible to distinguish truth from falsehood by seeking a multiplicity of views; just listening to a single view makes it impossible. One cannot manage anything on the basis of the urges of a moment; one should calm down and carefully consider in detail the true appearance of the other person involved. Thus, when hearing gossip about the doings of others, whether praise or condemnation, one should not blindly believe it. One can only distinguish the truth of anything through calm appraisal and consideration.

209. *The hot-tempered and coarse-minded will achieve nothing; a warm heart and calm air will attract good fortune.*

The proverb says: "The hasty-hearted cannot eat hot bean curd." Bean curd straight from the stove is piping hot and its flavor fills the air. It is easy to burn one's tongue when rushing to taste it and difficult to savor its flavor. Whether in study or in business one should concentrate one's will and keep one's temper for the sake of the end product. The *Great Learning*, one of the classic Confucian *Four Books*, says: "Stability and then calm, calm and then peace, peace and then thought, thought and then achievement." One can only become calm and unruffled once aspirations have been determined, only be at ease with oneself once calm, only capable of detailed thought once at ease, and only capable of achievement after detailed consideration. True achievement is only possible after one has become calm and considered the problem in a state of tranquility.

210. One should not treat underlings harshly, to do
so will cause those who might serve you to depart; one
should not be indiscriminate in the making of friends,
to do so will attract flatterers in search of favors.

In life, one should be openhearted in the treatment of
others and prudent in the making of friends. The proverb
says: "One kind word will bring warmth for three winters,
a single insult can freeze the month of June." Harsh words
and sarcasm will always distance people, so that in the end
one is utterly isolated and cut off, reliant upon one's own
paltry efforts in everything, and will find it difficult to
achieve success. The value of friendship lies in sincerity, not
in numbers. Friendship between gentlemen derives from
sincerity and an indifference to wealth and repute and thus
may appear by contrast to be insubstantial, refraining from
excitement and the unusual; it is nevertheless a situation of
mutual advantage.

*211. **In driving rain, secure your foothold; amidst the attractions of flowers and foliage, raise your eyes; on a precipitous track, turn to see the way back.***

One must stand firm in the face of the storms and dangers of life and be resolute in one's convictions. One should be openhearted and lofty in vision when confronted by temptation, that is the only way to avoid becoming confused and deluded. When a crisis is detected one should have the courage to withdraw so as to avoid being unable to extricate oneself from the quagmire of events. Difficulties and dangers occur on the journey through life; one should not fear difficulty or succumb but grasp one's own nature so that one is not sunk in confusion and delusion when things happen. The life of glory will always belong to those of lofty aspirations, resolute conviction and with the ability to seize the opportunity.

212. The character of the man of integrity must contain warmth of heart, only then can he avoid the path of dispute; the scholar of achievement must be filled with modesty and virtue, only then can the door to envy remain closed.

Those who fight for justice and redress wrongs are resolute in character but because of a tendency to disagreement they easily clash with others. Their strongpoint is a firm, even heroic, sense of resolve but their defect is a tendency to extremes of action. One should use the strengths of others to remedy one's own deficiencies and always be mindful of the need for warmheartedness to correct and moderate extreme conduct—the only way to avoid clashing with others. The proverb has it: "The wind will fell the tree taller than the wood, the crowd will take against conduct superior to the common man." The occupant of a position of eminence should comprehend that the permanence of any enterprise is only achieved by restraint in speech and action, modesty and prudence, the avoidance of bitter personal disputes, and the harnessing of one's energy to the performance of the tasks to be undertaken by oneself.

213. In office, the official does not casually entertain every recommendation for employment but makes himself difficult of access so as to avoid a stream of petitioners; in rural retirement he does not remain aloof but makes himself easy of access in order to promote neighborly relations.

Virtue in conduct has no relationship to status or position. In office one should maintain an attitude of prudent dignity in dealing with those who call seeking favors. One should maintain morality and purity of conduct, neither abandoning good manners nor ignoring the principles of the conduct of affairs, whilst still guarding against falling into the pit of fame and wealth. In retirement it is a case of: "If you do not occupy the post do not make its policy." Faced with elders and fellow villagers, one should be mild and moderate and be at one with the mass of people. If one retains an air of superiority, believing oneself to be a cut above the rest, it is very difficult to be at one with the collective and enjoy the warmth of communal life.

214. One cannot but revere the person of moral standing, in doing so one eliminates one's own indulgences; one cannot but revere the common man, in doing so one avoids a reputation for boorishness.

Confucius said: "The gentleman reveres three things: the Mandate of Heaven, people of moral standing and the sayings of the sages." Man must maintain reverence for the boundless universe and even for heaven, earth and nature. When confronted by the vastness of the universe and heaven and earth and the insignificance of mankind one should revere nature and respect its laws. Man must also respect the heroic ancestral causes of history. He must learn from the moral conduct of great historical figures and follow their example in forging ahead. Man should revere the words of the sages of the past even more. Knowledge should be respected and expanded. A man who possesses the qualities of reverence and an awareness of his own limitations will be neither ignorant nor recklessly unrestrained in the face of the affairs of the world.

215. When matters take an unfavorable turn, think of those less than oneself and you will no longer blame others; when the heart is at a low ebb, think of those superior to oneself and your spirits will revive.

Nothing in life is plain sailing and it is difficult to avoid losing one's footing on the way forward. Those who blame fate and others for their difficulties will only erode their will and courage to overcome difficulties in the process. At this point it does no harm to give thought to those not so well situated as oneself and in the comparison to look at one's own advantages and learn to value what one currently has. Hope will then be rekindled in the heart and once more energize the will to struggle on. By the same token, one should not be complacent at a little success but look at those superior to oneself and realize that one still has far to go. The ability to adjust one's feelings through comparison should enable you to manage problems more skillfully and strive for a better future.

216. In joy do not lightly make promises, in drink do not give way to anger, in impetuosity do not provoke trouble, in weariness do not start and never finish.

These are frequently encountered errors and should be guarded against. The truly perceptive person realizes the need for prudence in speech and action and does not lightly make promises, does not cause an incident when drunk, knows when to stop, and always completes a task. All this constitutes an admonition for the avoidance of error and regret.

217. The scholar should study until hands and feet dance with joy, only then will he avoid being trapped by lack of originality; the skilled observer should investigate until his mind becomes as one with the subject, only then will he not be mired in its outer appearance.

The importance of scholarship lies in an instinctive understanding and in the ability to grasp the inner meaning of a writer from within the text itself and then to apply it creatively. Things develop and circumstances change. Scholarship that is shackled by language and its script and lacks the spirit of independent thought and judgment becomes mere formalism without essence. The meaning and significance of observation lies in the merging of the subject with self, and its wonder lies in the combination of mind and subject into a single entity where self and subject are both forgotten. The Jin dynasty (265–420) poet Tao Yuanming (365 or 372 or 376–427) wrote:

> "I pluck the chrysanthemum bloom beneath the
>   eastern fence,
> And see serene the southern hills."

When the spirit of man achieves a high level of integration with the natural environment and merges self with heaven and earth, man will experience a breakthrough and considerably raise his state of awareness.

218. Heaven endows a man with the moral wisdom to enlighten the ignorance of other men, but to the contrary those in the world of today use their abilities to display other's faults; heaven enriches a man with the wealth to relieve the hardships of other men, but to the contrary those in the world of today employ all their possesses to humiliate others—true criminals in the eyes of heaven!

There are heights and depths to wisdom and ability and both more and less to wealth and riches. But the power and character bestowed upon man by nature are equal, so that no man has the right to despise others by reason of his own wealth or intelligence. Those with heaven-sent talent and extraordinary ability should shoulder the responsibility for contributing to society and seeking happiness for the people just as they use their intelligence and abilities to create a life of happiness for themselves. Merely seeking enjoyment for oneself or relying on one's own abilities to show off in front of those less well-endowed with wisdom and intelligence is to "seize the merits of heaven and turn them to one's own use." In the end, people will spurn such conduct.

219. The complete man knows whereof to think and what to consider, the ignorant man neither apprehends nor understands, but they may join in scholarly discussion and play a part in achievement. For the person of mediocre talent, the possession of a bit more knowledge and understanding and a bit more thought and doubt makes it difficult for them to set about anything.

Confucius said: "It is only the very wise and the very stupid who may not be changed." In life, exceptionally clever people filled with wisdom get to the root of everything, see things for what they are, are resolute in character and are not disturbed by external material influences. The stupid and straightforward, armed with self-knowledge, simplehearted and pure minded, are also less corruptible. Only these two types of people are both pure and resolute by nature. Both pitiable and contemptible are those who waver in the middle, not very wise yet not without acumen, who rack their brains in the pursuit of profit and repute, who exhaust every device and yet, in the end, achieve nothing.

220. The mouth is the door to the heart, if the mouth is not closely guarded, one's innermost secrets will leak; consciousness and intention are the feet of the heart, if they are not well guarded they will march the road of evil to its end.

First, in one's conduct in life the mouth should be as tightly stoppered as a bottle. Second, one should be resolute in will. The proverb says: "Disaster emerges from the mouth." A moment of thoughtless speech in which words that should not be spoken carelessly escape may cause damage that is difficult to put right and will have serious consequences. Only a genuine realization of the significance of one's speech will enable one to avoid such consequences. Resolution of will requires a long period of arduous toughening and rigorous testing but as long as one's aim remains clear, one strives subjectively and is sufficiently confident, then one will achieve steadfastness of character, control of oneself, resistance to temptation and will never take the crooked road.

221. In one's demands upon others, find the faultless amongst the faults and there will be tranquility of feeling; in one's demands upon oneself, seek the faults within the faultless and morality will enter.

It is often said that man has two eyes, one on others and one on himself. Chinese traditional culture advocates: "Harshness for oneself, leniency for others," and, "In contemplation consider one's own faults, in conversation never discuss the misdeeds of others." One should make strict demands of oneself and frequently reflect upon one's own shortcomings in order to achieve continuous progress and improvement. When there are problems one should seek the cause in oneself and not blame others. One should be generous and forgiving in the treatment of others and when they make mistakes remind them gently rather than exaggerate and indulge in trivial faultfinding.

222. The newborn babe is father to the man, the graduate is the foundation of the minister. Thus, if pottery is badly fired at the start, it will not make a true vessel and later in life and at court there will be no real talent.

The *Three Character Classic* (so called because each phrase consists of just three characters), a traditional work of instruction for children says: "Unworked jade cannot make a fashioned object; without study you will not know righteousness." There is no successful undertaking imaginable that does not require diligent and persevering effort. The ancients said: "Fail to strive when young and healthy and old age will be a sorrow." Everything requires the earliest possible planning and the most adequate preparation. Each and every new step needs additional effort.

223. The gentleman may be unconcerned by adversity but should be vigilant when taking his pleasure; he should be unafraid in the face of power but shocked by isolation.

Poverty and riches, power and position are circumstances external to oneself and unrelated to one's nature. Where his nature is uninfluenced by the external world, the gentleman is untroubled by adversity and courageously and positively pushes forward in the face of the trials and tribulations of life. In a life of ease and pleasure, the gentleman must have a clearheaded realization of the philosophical principle that "living derives from adversity." He continuously hones his will and guards against confusion and corruption. He upholds righteousness and lacks the rogue's expression of flattery towards superiors and contempt for those beneath. In the face of a bully he is brave and fearless. When he comes across the impoverished he does all that he can to help them. This is the character and nature of a gentleman.

224. The peach and plum may be splendid, but
what of the unswerving loyalty of pine and cypress?
Apricot and pear may be sweet, but what of the sharp
fragrance of tangerine and orange? So it is! Passing
beauty cannot exceed the simple and long-lasting; early
grace is not better than late maturity.

The *Analects* says: "When cold winter comes, it is then you know that pine and cypress are the last to wither." Peach red and willow green may blaze in beauty for a while but they cannot match the green longevity of pine and cypress. When all the flowers have withered, the jade-green of pine and cypress shines forth all the more brightly amidst the wind and the rain, the snow and the ice. Peach and apricot ripen early and taste sweet but they are soon out of season; tangerine and orange ripen late, their taste plain and refined but they last longer. Life is the same. There are people who achieve success early and others who mature into success. The successful young easily become arrogant and resemble flowers that blossom only once; the mature are refined into steel and can last much longer.

225. It is through a tranquil mind that you may discover the true condition of life; it is through plain living that you may perceive the original mind and body.

The Tang dynasty poet Li She (dates unknown) wrote:
> "By a bamboo court I meet a monk,
> From whose lips I gain
> The consolation of half a day."

With a tranquil mind one may put all one's heart into study, achieve in learning, and grow in ability and competence. Only with a tranquil mind can one's spirit be concentrated and perceptions deepened. Only in a life of unhurried peace and tranquility is it possible to regain one's original unaltered state of true self, to comprehend the true essence of life, to enjoy peace and ease and the beauty of spiritual peace.

226. Those who envy the hermit's life may not necessarily gain its joy; those who condemn talk of fame and profit may not necessarily have utterly forgotten their attractions.

There are many things in which reality and appearance are far apart. Those who, on the face of it, appear to envy the carefree life of the hermit in the hills may not feel in their bones that they really appreciate that kind of life. Those who really understand the reclusive life moved to the hills long ago and stayed there. Lingche (746–816) the poet-monk of the middle of the Tang dynasty wrote:

> "As to those who meet and say
> How nice to give up office,
> In the world of streams and woods,
> Whoever met such a man?"

Similarly, it is possible that those loud in their condemnation of fame and profit may, deep in their bones, feel a burning desire for it. Consequently, to achieve a clear assessment of somebody, one should disregard what they say, however splendid it may be, and observe what they actually do.

227. Fishing is a matter of leisure, yet one holds the rod of life and death; chess is an elegant game, but the mind moves in aggressive strategy. Thus, we may see that it is better to be unoccupied than occupied and that the utter truth of lack of talent is better than talent by the multitude.

In Chinese traditional culture, Buddhism teaches compassion and Daoism seeks non-action. Seen this way, although fishing and chess are both recreational pursuits, they contain the seeds of both murder and war that not only encourage the act of killing but also stimulate the cunning needed to win battles. This kind of behavior and mentality is of no help at all in nurturing a character that is both honest and tolerant.

228. Flowering blossom filling hills and valleys with beauty, that has always been a worldly illusion; when the trees wither and the water falls to expose the jagged rocks, that is when you see your true self.

In spring, the flowers blossom, birds fly, the grass grows and the wooded hills are filled with an atmosphere of burgeoning nature. In winter, however, the leaves wither, bird and beast hide away, and in a moment hills and forest turn bleak and chilly; that is their original appearance. When you survey the long history of society, riches and honor vanish like a puff of smoke. Better to return to the purity and reality of one's inner mind than to struggle in the vortex of right and wrong; better to accept the truth and virtue of heaven and mankind with a pure and receptive heart.

*229. The years and months stretch out, but the busy
man drives himself on; heaven and earth are vast, but
the small-minded man keeps to himself; wind, flowers,
snow and moon exist in leisure, but the exhausted man
believes them superfluous.*

Buddhism teaches: "Sun and moon shine bright but the
blind do not see them." The beauty of heaven and earth
selflessly appears before everyone, but we lack a sense of
appreciation and an aesthetic sense with which to judge
it, becoming both blind and deaf, neither able to hear nor
see the beauty. We busy ourselves making a living, striving
after fame and profit, and all that is left to us in the world
is a life of ceaseless rushing about. We are in no mood to
appreciate or enjoy even the most beautiful scenery—
that little piece of poetic satisfaction in our hearts quietly
slipped away long ago.

230. The joy of something does not lie in how much or how many, mountain mists may just as much hang over a fistful of pebbles in a basin of water; scenery is not a matter of distance, its beauty is there to be seen through a plain bamboo window.

There is scenery everywhere in life, each blade of grass and every tree worthy of attention. The beauty and delight of life does not lie in the how much or how many of material things or the amount of wealth or the sheer scale of things but in an innate understanding and inner contentment. Life's joy is hidden in life itself, we have only to put our mind to discovering it and we will find it at our side. Buddhism teaches: "Each flower a world and each leaf a Buddha." If Buddha is in the heart then all that we see is infused with a sense of the Buddha. The richness of the spirit is not determined by a material hierarchy, nor is elegance of tone or mood determined by wealth or lack of it. A free and noble soul will naturally possess the uninhibited freedom of movement of clouds and water.

231. The sound of a bell in the stillness of night wakes us from the illusory dream within the dream; through the reflection of the moon in still water we glimpse the true body that is beyond our body.

The *Diamond Sutra* teaches: "All that exists is unreal and an illusion." In the eyes of Buddhism, all living things are ever changing and impermanent, dreams and fantasies. Through the sound of the distant bell in the stillness of night, or the illusory sight of flowers in a mirror or the moon in water, we are more than ever able to comprehend the traceless and indistinct nature of the illusions of man and the universe. If, in a state of silent clarity, one can perceive calmly, then one can awake from the midst of a great dream and realize what really is the true life of one's spiritual nature.

232. The call of birds and the sound of insects express their inner secrets; in the beauty of flowers and the lushness of grass we may perceive the Way. The man of learning must comprehend the mysteries of heaven and wisdom of man and reach out with an open heart to the knowledge and understanding contained in all things.

"To understand the ways of the world is knowledge indeed, to be experienced in the ways of men is a virtue." This is true of human society and also of the natural world. Through sun, moon and stars, flowers, birds, fish and insects, wind, rain, thunder and lightning, man comprehends the myriad changes and transformations of the natural world. Unfortunately, most human hearts are filled with the desire for fame and profit and lack any awareness of the Buddhist mysteries contained within nature. However, for those who cultivate learning, the key to awareness lies in purity of heart and mind and it is only this quality that will enable one to comprehend the almost pictorial detail of the truths of the Way to be found in nature.

233. Man can only make out text that contains writing, he cannot read text that contains no writing; he can only pluck a qin *that has strings, he cannot play a* qin *that has none. This is an attachment to matter that has form, not knowledge of the formless. How may one then grasp the formless sense of both text and* qin?

The nature and wisdom of man lies in intention and awareness. Once fettered by external forms he loses his innate quickness of mind and purity of nature. If one is unable to comprehend this unwritten sutra of life, how will one be able to grasp the true meaning of that written text? If one is unable to play the stringless *qin* (Chinese ancient musical instrument), how will one be able to appreciate the wonderful sound of both text and *qin*? The true aesthetic state is only achieved through transcending the outward appearance of things to reach and take in their inner spirits. It is only through knowledge of the outward appearance of social life and then seeing through appearances to the fundamental nature of things that one may become truly aware of the total significance of life.

234. A heart without material desire is like the clear sky of autumn or the sea after rain; seated with qin *and text is to be transported to a fairy world of jeweled dwellings and cinnabar hills.*

Mengzi wrote: "There is no better way of nurturing the mind than by a diminution of desire." It is one's greed and desire that are most able to deceive one's original mind and basic nature. We can only achieve a mind as clear and lofty as an autumn sky through controlling the flow of desire and stilling the distractions of the clamorous world so that we can enjoy a spiritual peace, free of care. In life it is better to enjoy the leisured company of *qin* and text than to pass every day mired in sex and drunkenness.

235. A meeting of friends and guests is a time of drink and revelry, but time runs out and the candles gutter, the incense burns away and the tea grows cold, making all nauseous and insipid. The world too is like this; how can one have failed to look back earlier?

The Emperor Wu of Han (156–87 BC) once said: "Extreme joy brings much sorrow." Taken to extremes things move in reverse. The exciting moment of glory soon turns swiftly and inevitably to loneliness and desolation. The glory of the thronged courtyard turns to emptiness where only sparrows are seen and weeds flourish. Thus, we can see that there is no permanence to this world and that rise and fall follow each other in succession. We should not place our hopes for joy and happiness upon the superficial bustle and busyness of life, otherwise, the higher we aim the further we fall and the greater the psychological blow.

236. Gain the essential appeal of something and all the
vastness of the world itself enters the heart; seize the
mystery before one's eyes and the heroes of antiquity
are within your grasp.

No matter what, once learned from experience,
everything, be it sun, moon, hills or rivers, will all join
and breath as one with your soul. No matter what human
reason or cause, once its inner principle is perceived,
heroes ancient and modern will serve you. Man lives
between heaven and earth and once he has learned the
spiritual sense of the beauty of hills and rivers, he may
then sufficiently comprehend the appeal of nature. Man,
once he has used his intelligence to plumb the mysteries
of human nature, may improve his strategies sufficiently to
cope with life.

237. Rivers, mountains and the earth itself are of dust already, how much more the dust within the dust? Flesh, blood and the body itself are as bubbles and shadows, how much more the shadow beyond the shadow? If there is no wisdom, there can be no mind to comprehend it.

Time flies but the hills remain. The great figures and their heroic deeds have long departed in dust and smoke. In the face of limitless time and space, man is as negligible as the particles of dust that go to make up dust or the shadows within a shadow. How can one see through to the fundamental principle in all this without an alert intelligence? The man who truly lives a life that is spiritually penetrating and unimpeded has no need to accept the anxiety caused by changes of mood or to remain entangled and unable to escape from the trammels of love and hate or passion and animosity. He may lightly and easily follow his heart's desire to the life that he seeks. This ideal state of life is one that is untroubled and free of care. Thus, the wise man is able to see through and also to let go.

238. As we struggle to and fro in the brief light of a spark, how much time is really left? As we battle to the death on the horns of a snail, how big is the world truly?

Life is both short and bitter—as short as the morning dew, or the spark from a flint or a flash of lightning. Thus, we must never waste valuable time, or fritter away our precious life in vain. Time is valuable and in a life of limited length we must use our energy to do things that are significant and worthwhile. Time is valuable, it should not be wasted in feeling sorry for ourselves or in feeling uneasy or in pain, each day should be joyful and not passed in suffering.

239. There is no flame to a cold candle nor warmth to worn furs, all is upside down. The body is a dead tree and the spirit burnt ashes; there can be no avoiding a descent into the void of desolation.

The impoverished life is no warm bed for the practice of the Way nor is a withered soul the master of enlightenment. The void as described in Buddhism is by no means empty of everything; it brims with vitality. It is merely the one-sided advocacy of a life of shabby clothing and an empty stomach that makes the heart seeking the Way seem like dead wood and burnt ashes—it suffocates people and saps their vitality. Consequently, those who practice the Way should beware of becoming obsessed with the descent into the void. They should experience the warmth of the world with a lively and independent spirit, value the beauty of humanity, and treat life with a little more compassionate love.

240. If a man wishes to rest at once then rest he should. If always first seeking a resting place before taking a rest, remember that there is more in marriage than just the wedding; the path of the monk may be calm but his mind will always be busy. Our forebears said: "Rest when you will, wait till all is done and you will wait forever." Behold their wisdom!

The proverb says: "Don't decide when you should decide and you will bear the consequences." Once you have made up your mind, act at once, it is the sharp knife that cuts the Gordian knot. Always wait for the right time or the right opportunity and you will wait forever. Don't go looking for excuses for yourself, in the end it will always be a case of "today always becomes tomorrow and how many tomorrows are there?" When is the best time? At once is the best time. So you must grasp the moment and act on the instant. Being endlessly entangled in events means that worry and anxiety will follow on your heels.

241. Observe the hot from the cold and you will know the uselessness of the heat of repute and position; proceed from busyness to leisure and you will sense that its flavor is the longer lasting.

There are all kinds of situations in life and if one does not break free of one's original shackles to undertake profound self-examination, how can one come to know their flavor or penetrate their mysteries? One's attitude towards power and wealth should be cool-headed and self-controlled. Being content and happy with one's lot is a kind of wisdom, and indifference to fame and fortune is a mental state. Both can help those adrift in the sea of desire obtain some comfort from the petty anxieties of work and a little peace amidst restlessness. Consequently, the open-minded man will always seek spiritual independence and keep his distance from the hubbub of the mundane world.

242. Wear wealth and repute as lightly as a cloud and there will be no need to dwell amongst hills and caves; for those without a craving for rocks and springs, to drink wine and recite poetry is enough.

One should seek the reality rather than the form. One should not fall into error because of the pursuit of a particular form. Some say that a hermit's life is a craving for rocks and springs and others that the refined life is the abandoning of wealth. In fact, the decisive factor is a matter of temperament. Provided that the concept of a more than ordinary freedom from the mundane exists in the mind there is no necessity to seek out deep mountains and distant ravines to cultivate mind and body. Although the ancients always chose somewhere secluded to practice cultivation—for the most part deep mountains and remote ravines—people today lack the opportunity to move to remote locations in order to practice, thus, they should be aware of the following principle: life everywhere is a place of Buddhist or Daoist contemplation where one may practice all the time. The key is the utter jettisoning of one's own inner sense of greed.

243. Let others compete, do not resent their intoxication with wealth and repute; calm indifference may suit oneself but do not boast that only you are aware. This is what Shakyamuni Buddha called "neither entangled by cause nor trapped in the void, both body and spirit existing unhindered."

To be virtuous and then flaunt one's virtue or wise and then ridicule others is to debase virtue and turn wisdom to stupidity. Living in the world we need to be quietly contented but not insipid, to harbor ambition but not be blind in its pursuit. We should observe the rules but not be shackled by them. We should live a simple life but this should not mean that we do nothing at all. Not to be in competition with the world or contaminated by it is to be secluded in spirit despite living in the mundane world.

244. The long and short of time is but a perception of the mind and the breadth or narrowness of space is a matter of mood. Thus, for those who can seize the moment of leisure a single day may last forever, and for those with breadth of vision the tiny chamber may seem a spacious hall.

Time is both the shortest and longest thing in the world. Buddhism teaches that all phenomena are creations of the mind. The happy person may feel that just a moment of a good night is worth thousands and that there is not enough time. For the man of misery, a day may seem like a year with every moment spent in torment. The moment of leisure snatched from the busy life lasts a thousand years; with breadth of vision the humble hut appears a palace. One should always examine and review one's state of mind and not permit oneself to be controlled by one's surroundings, thus losing the initiative. Expand the mind, do not take things too seriously and one will be content; if one is unable to let go, then the mind will be filled with pent-up frustration. Accommodate the whole world within the space of a square inch and one will be able to face life boldly.

*245. Diminish desire and then diminish again, pluck
flowers and plant bamboo and consign all vexation
to oblivion. Forget to the point where there is nothing
that can be forgotten. Burn incense and make tea and
think not of the white-clad bearers of wine.*

Daoism teaches: "The Way is achieved by daily diminution."
That is, comprehension of the Way is achieved by a
process of reduction in which desire is diminished and
then diminished again, the greedy attachment to fame,
advantage and wealth is abandoned, and one attains a
state of selflessness. In one's leisure one may do a little
gardening, burn incense, taste tea and take a little wine,
and clear the brain of all vexation and anxiety. The life
plainly lived has its own quiet and simple flavor.

246. For those that know contentment, all that lies before their eyes is a fairyland; for those that know it not, it is utterly ordinary. Everything arises from the causes of the world; for those skilled in their use they are life's opportunities but to the unskilled they are a danger.

The *Daodejing* says: "To know contentment is a constant joy." The desires of men know no limit and it is only knowledge of contentment and contentment with one's lot that will enable one to truly gain happiness. No matter how much wealth a man may possess, if he is forever immersed in the torment and suffering of the struggle for fame and riches and the frenzy of activity, he is actually no different in essence from the poor. If we allow our desires to spread unchecked, we shall never escape the trap of the mundane world. We must be skilled in grasping the many opportunities and relationships of life. If we let these opportunities slip, then not only will there be no miracles, it will have an influence on the next stage of any undertaking as well.

247. The disasters that arise from proximity to power are both tragic and rapid; the flavor of leisured tranquility is milder and lasts longer.

Because they enjoy material advantages and spiritual sensations that the ordinary man can only dream of, men of power are always surrounded by a crowd of hangers on. But proximity to power is rather like embracing disaster; the city gate may catch fire at any moment and spread to the fishpond. Thus, those who are not obsessed with fame and profit and do not seek the company of the powerful may, because of the happiness due to their distance from disaster, pass each day in freedom and contentment and achieve the longest lasting happiness of all. Consequently, when faced with the illusions of power, wealth and fame, we should accept them with a tolerant smile knowing that behind them stands nothing that is particularly exceptional. Only by not being moved by fame, riches and honor can we achieve wisdom and become optimistic and independent, and suffer less grief and anxiety.

248. With staff in hand, walk alone under the pines by the stream. Stand with the clouds forming around your tattered gown. Lean, pillowed on a book beneath a bamboo window and as you doze, the moonlight floods across the chilly quilt.

In his poem *A Hermit's Life in Zhongnan* the Tang dynasty poet Wang Wei (701–761) wrote:

> "…When fancy strikes I stroll alone,
> Drunk with joy of sight and sound,
> To water's head and seated watch the furling
>   clouds …"

What he describes is a kind of state that is in tune with nature, is contented and at ease and faces the vicissitudes of life calmly. Those caught up in the hurly-burly of the mundane life should relax. The leisured life of hills and woods amidst wild cranes and lazily drifting cloud is difficult to attain, but there one may discard a little of the dust of the mundane world. This kind of peaceful tranquility is difficult to achieve and enjoy for those worldly characters bent on fame and profit.

249. Carnal lust is like a blazing fire, but think of a sickened body and it seems like cold ashes; fame and profit are like sweet syrup but think of death and they seem like chewing candles. Consequently, people often worry about illness and death, for the thought can dispel illusions and increase virtue.

Wealth and position can create a yearning that when unattainable is the cause of vexation and suffering. At this point it does no harm to think of the hereafter; those fine garments and that precious jewelry, which of it can one take with one? In illness one thinks of the emptiness and tragedy of life and at death's door survival may be the only thought left. Consequently, in order to prevent endless misfortune, one should normally face the facts and consider the problem, rather than do as one pleases or behave as one wants.

250. The path of competition is narrow, step back a pace and it becomes wider; heavy flavors do not last, a little lighter and they will last longer.

The ancients often said: "Draw back a step and the heavens will open and the sea will expand, a moment of patience and the wind will drop and the waves abate." Man must progress actively and strive upwards but he must also have a generous and tolerant heart and the insight to know when to take stock of a situation. It is when people struggle with each other to cross a narrow bridge that things are at their most dangerous. Giving people room is also to give oneself room. There are thousands of roads through life and therefore no need to crowd along the same path. Step back a pace and consider things calmly; that other track is a wide new path. There is bitter, hot, sweet and sour to life. There are people who like a life of rich gorgeous flavors but they should know that magnificence carried to excess will revert to ordinary dullness! The ordinary life is the true life.

251. To avoid confusion when busy, you must be
clearheaded when at leisure; to avoid fear in the face
of death, you must perceive the mysteries of life.

The sense of determination that prevents panic in the face
of danger is built up, little by little, drop by drop over the
course of daily life. During times of leisure, do not relax
the honing of the will but constantly maintain clarity and
agility of mind, so that if a sudden emergency arises you
may deal with it calmly. Those who cling to the earthly life
have a particular fear of death. Thus, during life they must
have the wisdom to perceive the mysteries of life and death
so that as death approaches they may face both life and
death calmly and at ease.

252. Hermits dwelling in the forests and hills are beyond honor and disgrace; following the Way one is beyond the hot and cold fickleness of the world.

Daoism promotes withdrawal from the world, this is why hermits completely discard the worldly notions of right and wrong and are without the senses of honor and disgrace. As Daoists see it, the secular world's concept of shame and honor is as insubstantial and illusory as flowers seen in a mirror or the moon reflected in water. If we thirst after the fame and wealth of the red dust of the secular world, we easily become prone to anxiety about loss and gain. If we battle with each other in the maelstrom of reputation and riches, we become exceptionally sensitive to the fickleness of human relationships. If, in the hubbub of the red dust of the secular world, we can transcend the muddy currents of material desire, then we will be able to forget loss and gain and strengthen our belief in the search for the Way. What matters then the approval or disapproval of others?

253. We cannot do without heat, but we must do away with the heat of vexation so that we feel as if our body is at ease on a cool terrace; we cannot do away with poverty, but we must do away with the worries of poverty so that our mind is nested in comfort.

The raging heat of high summer cannot be compared with the fires of the mind. No way out cannot be compared with utter despair. Zhuangzi said: "There is no greater sadness than a lifeless heart." There is no greater tragedy in life than despair and negativity of thought. There is nothing to be frightened of in even the most desperate of external situations, what is important is how you yourself face up to it. It is impossible to avoid the physical distress of heat but the suffering of the mental fires of lust must be eradicated. There is nothing to be feared from material poverty. It is optimism of spirit that is true wealth. If you face everything in a positive spirit then you hold the key to happiness.

254. As one advances so should one think of withdrawal in order to avoid the disaster of being trapped; as one grasps so should one first think of how to let go so as to avoid the dangers of riding a tiger.

Laozi said: "Disaster is the buttress of fortune and fortune is the crumbling of disaster." When things are going favorably and one's career is a success, one must take account of the hidden risks and give oneself a way out so as to avoid the fate of the goat trapped in a fence, able neither to push forward nor to pull back. When all is going well in life and everything one touches turns to gold, then is the time to be alert and recognize the moment to disengage, otherwise it will be like riding a tiger—when one thinks of getting down, it is already too late.

255. The avaricious gain gold but covet jade and become ministers but complain of not being ennobled, and rich and powerful families regard themselves as poor as beggars; the contented believe pigweed better than grain and a cloth gown warmer than fox fur. In this, why should the common people yield in spirit to princes and dukes?

The insatiably greedy receive an inch and demand a foot, seize one land and covet the next. Their desires are like a bottomless pit, impossible to fill. Even when they lead the life of royalty or nobility, they are like beggars in mind, incapable of satisfaction. A person is happy not because his possessions are so many but because his external demands are so few. Poverty and riches do not depend upon the more or less of material wealth but upon whether or not there is satisfaction of spirit. Treasure all that you have and happiness will be before your eyes.

256. It is better to flee the trappings of fame than to flaunt them, better the ease of less involvement than skill in the practice of affairs.

Shallow water flows noisily but still waters are deep. The self-possessed and cultivated person even though he may enjoy wealth and reputation will not use it as capital for self-display, forgetting himself and flaunting it in a domineering exhibition of fame and power. On the contrary, he will know himself well and will respond to public adulation in a subdued and modest manner and retain his natural qualities and original nature. "The gentleman is filled with virtue but has the modest aspect of ignorance." A gentleman behaves with an open mind and hides his light beneath a bushel.

257. Lovers of solitude have but to look at clouds and crags and can fathom the mysteries of the universe; lovers of excitement have but to see song and dance and then forget their fatigue. For the contented, neither solitary nor noisy, neither glorious nor decrepit, there is nowhere that is unsuited.

People are not all the same in character and nature, and life consists of many kinds. One may be a hermit living a tranquil, unhurried life in the company of blue mountains and green streams. One may also achieve success in the field of fame and riches. For the self-possessed, optimistic man there is no difference between lifestyles; they can all live in happiness and contentment. Consequently, one must cultivate optimism in one's own life and not set one's heart on any one particular thing. If one takes everything as it comes there will naturally be less anxiety.

258. The single cloud floating free of the mountain peaks comes and goes at will; the full moon as bright as a mirror hanging in the sky shines upon both beauty and ugliness without distinction.

The weary bird returns to its nest; the official exhausted by bureaucracy returns to the countryside. Whether to go or to stay is entirely a response to opportunity, there is no force involved whatsoever. When, through practice, one's wisdom has reached a certain level, one would not seek the favor of the king before one, or treat a beggar with disdain, or lust after jewels displayed before one's eyes or avoid the dog shit in one's way. One would be aware of them but make no distinction between them.

259. The flavor that lasts lies not in strong liquor but in the simple taste of plain vegetables and clear water; feelings of regret are not born of withered solitude but of the bustle and hubbub of life. Thus it is that one perceives the brevity of strong flavors and that simple flavors are the only true ones.

Fireworks soon grow cold and fine views do not last. The flavor of life does not reside in delicate food and fine wine but in the drop-by-drop passage of daily life.

260. Zen tells us: "Eat when hungry, sleep when tired." The poem has it: "Plain language will describe the grand scenery before you." Thus it is that the sublime resides in the pedestrian and that the difficult is to be found within the easy; those with intent will always be distant from this truth, the spontaneous will always find it close at hand.

There are too many people in the world who eat and guzzle, drink and swill, who sleep uneasily, their minds in turmoil. In truth, eating and sleeping are the most commonplace and ordinary of life's activities. In the same way, those who pursue an occupation without intent are, by contrast, closer to a natural innocence and from it derive an almost unimaginable strength. In this world it has always been: "Pluck flowers with intent and they blossom not, plant willows by accident and they will provide shade." Those who pursue with intent never achieve their aim but for those who strive without premeditation it may arrive naturally.

*261. Water flows but the rocks are silent, thus one may
see the charm of quiet in a noisy place; mountains are
high but clouds float free, thus one may comprehend
the mysteries of the void.*

Wang Ji (dates unknown), a poet of the Southern dynasties
(420–589) wrote:

> "Cicadas drone,
>
> The forest seems quieter still.
>
> Birds sing
>
> And the hills are more remote."

Not only does the noise of birds and cicadas fail to disturb,
somehow it sets off the seclusion of hills and forests. A
state of mind in which it is possible to maintain silence
amidst the hubbub of the red dust demonstrates a degree
of cultivation extremely difficult to achieve. If one can
forget one's surroundings, then one can ignore their noise
and clamor. Mastering the ability to forget is not difficult.
If one can avoid an attachment to a certain kind of form
and not covet fame and wealth, then it is possible to
achieve a state of self-oblivion and non-being (*anatta*). If
one forgets the pretensions of the external material world,
then naturally they cannot ensnare the mind. However
complicated things may be, one's spirit will remain free
and at ease.

262. Hills and forests are places of great beauty but once there is selfish attachment, they become a common marketplace; calligraphy and painting are things of elegance but once there is a desire for possession, they become commodities. Thus it is that to the pure in heart the world of desire is a mere fairyland but to those possessed by desire, joy becomes a sea of suffering.

To those whose minds are undisturbed, their ancestral village can be anywhere, to those whose minds cannot settle, prison is all around. To the cultivated man, hills and forests, calligraphy and painting are close friends and companions, tranquil and simple, carefree and at ease; to the industriously rich and famous they are arenas, commercial opportunities and places of cutthroat competition and struggle. From this can be seen that elegant or atrocious taste is not enshrined in the physical object itself but in one's state of mind.

263. In times of noise and confusion, one's memories of ordinary times become lost in vagueness; in times of tranquility, memories long neglected vividly reappear. Thus, it can be seen that the slightest difference between calm and agitation may mean all the difference between confusion and clarity.

People who are impetuous by nature are often clumsy and careless in their handling of events, they frequently forget things and are generally negligent. Those of a calm frame of mind think carefully, act conscientiously and succeed easily. The Confucian classic, the *Book of Rites* says: "With a clear mind in the body, resolve will be supernatural." Calm and tranquility of mind can bring clarity of wisdom. The resolve that enables someone to face danger calmly is an expression of the effort they put into maintaining tranquility.

264. Beneath a quilt of reeds, bedded in snow and asleep within the clouds one preserves the shelter of the night; clasping a cup of bamboo, reciting to the wind and teasing the moon is a refuge far distant from the red dust.

In his *Record of the Pavilion of the Drunken Old Man*, Ouyang Xiu (1007–1072) wrote: "The joy of a landscape of hills and water may be grasped by the heart and found in wine." The charm of touring by hill and water lies especially in a leisured and carefree spirit. The natural landscape contains none of the falseness and deceit of the mundane world. To be able to linger amongst the scenery, to lie amongst clouds and sleep with the moon, to abandon the commonplace and transcend the dust of the mundane world, then truly one may say: "All is well with the world."

265. In the midst of pomp and circumstance, were a hermit with a staff to appear, that would add a touch of elegance; amongst fisherfolk and woodcutters, were a splendidly attired courtier to appear, that would add a layer of vulgarity. Thus, one knows that luxury is not the master of the plain and simple and that vulgarity does not rival elegance.

Past and present, within and without, the political stage has always bristled with thorns, and traps lie set everywhere. What is it that really lies beneath the splendid attire of the courtier; really how many pure spirits are there? It is easy to retain sincerity of conduct in the plain and simple life of the hill dweller. This sincerity in social relationships is an indispensable quality in conduct and behavior. Whether it is the scholar of halls and courts or the sages of mountains and fields, what one finally sees is the character of the man.

*266. The Way from the world lies within the world
itself, there is no need to cut oneself off from mankind
in order to escape; the comprehension of the heart
lies deep within the heart itself, there is no need to
extinguish desire and shrivel the heart.*

The Zen Master Huineng (638–713) said: "The law of
Buddha is of this world, it is to be understood within the
world." Buddhist practice is practice within the world and
its proofs are to be found within the life of man. The world
is immense and limitless in splendor. As long as Buddha is
within the heart then all and everywhere is Buddha. To flee
the world in search of Buddha is an unattainable quest. This
is why it is said that there is no practice beyond the world
and that the heart is tempered through experience.

In the cultivation of mind and body the key is to
observe a person's inner heart; the amount of control
that it possesses governs their extent and ability to
practice. Seeking the form alone is rather like fishing for
compliments. Hence one must do one's utmost to seek to
understand life and comprehend the wisdom of life that
lies in ordinary life.

267. A body at ease is not trapped by ideas of honor or shame, gain or loss; a mind in tranquility is not deceived by ideas of advantage or disadvantage, right or wrong.

People who lust after wealth and success, once situated amidst honor or shame, benefit or cost, advantage or disadvantage, right or wrong, often find themselves anxious about problems of loss and gain and find it difficult to sleep well. This kind of life is a torment and a worry. Consequently, living in the red dust of the mundane world requires a relaxed mood like that of clouds and water in which matters of reputation and profit are regarded rather more lightly. This is the only way to avoid the snares of desire; allow one's spirit to maintain a state of tranquility and right and wrong will become absolutely and naturally apparent.

268. Suddenly hear cocks crow or dogs bark by a bamboo fence and you are at once transported to a fairy world in the clouds; hear by chance the drone of cicadas or the chatter of swallows at the window of your study and know the workings of the universe.

Zhuge Liang once said: "Without tranquility there can be no reaching into the distance." That is to say, unless there is tranquility of body and mind there is no way that far-reaching ideals may be achieved. No matter whether sages or common people, all may nurture wisdom and knowledge when in a state of tranquility. In a study or by a bamboo fence, each has its own secluded scenery. Listen to dogs bark and cocks crow, the cicadas drone and the swallows chatter and they unconsciously pluck at your heartstrings. Amongst the hills and waters of the seeming fairyland and within the study, a realm of tranquility enshrines all the beauty and every changing aspect of nature.

269. I do not hope for glory, why therefore should I be tempted by the flavor of profit and riches? I do not struggle to advance, why therefore should I fear the perils of the official life?

When the empire prospers, all arrive because of advantage; when the empire is in chaos, all depart because of advantage. The field of fame and wealth harbors great disaster, but in the face of calamity the choice of disaster is one that you make yourself. How can the fish be hooked if it is not greedy for that momentary delicacy? If you are not ambitious for wealth and fame how can you be tossed to and fro in the sea of official life? Consequently, if you wish to live your life in peace, you must work obediently, keep to your place and store up reward for a long, peaceful and stable life.

270. Wander amongst the rocks and springs of mountain and forest and the red dust gradually disappears; pause amongst poetry and painting and the commonplace will vanish. So it is that although the gentleman may not lose resolve through indulgence in the physical world, he often borrows from it to succor his soul.

Xunzi said: "The gentleman need choose to dwell in the country and should associate with scholars, thus protecting himself from the crooked and bringing himself closer to uprightness." Those who find themselves in an elegant and refined environment filled with an atmosphere of scholarship absorbed through long contact will naturally be imperceptibly influenced. Wandering the landscape of hills and streams, composing poetry and painting pictures nurtures one's nature and refines body and mind. Fusion with nature will harmonize body with mind and bring joy.

271. The burgeoning weather of spring invigorates the worn out spirit but it cannot surpass the white cloud and mists of autumn, the fragrance of orchids, where water and sky are of one color, bright above and below, that purify body and soul.

In spring everything revives, birds chatter and flowers are scented and all is full of life. Autumn represents ripeness and reaping. Even more, the weather is fine and clear and raises the spirits. Man's like or dislike of scenery is also based on mood and attitude. There must be both rise and fall in the lives of all living things. As with the four seasons, spring is the youth of man and autumn represents maturity. The adult has experienced much and harvested both wisdom and stability. When recalling his youth, he cannot but feel that it somehow lacked experience. In this sense it might be said that the flourishing vigor of spring cannot equal the bright clarity of autumn. However, if there is no spring of inexperienced youth, where then is the stability of autumn?

272. Not to be able to write a word but to be imbued with poetry, that is the true meaning of being a poet; not to have studied a single verse but to have the instinct of Zen, that is to truly comprehend its mysteries.

Life is a great book that contains classics that are written and classics that are unwritten. The Zen school advocates "Ignore the texts, see into one's nature and become a Buddha," believing that spirituality in life does not depend upon whether or not one is literate but upon whether or not one can see through to one's original nature. The principle of life and even the very profundity of wisdom lies only in whether or not one can grasp its very essence and avoid any relationship with external appearance or form. It is only by single-minded practice and conscious self-awareness that one can make a contribution. Zen meditation is like this, Daoist comprehension is like this, and there is neither poetry nor painting that is not like this.

273. The person of deceitful intent will see a serpent in the shadow of a bow or a crouching tiger in the shape of a sleeping stone, into all this a murderous nature is mixed; for those in whom such thoughts have ceased, the stone tiger will be a seagull and the croaking of frogs will be the sound of music and life will be everywhere.

Buddhism teaches that: "All phenomena are a manifestation of consciousness." Thus, good and evil are contained within a single thought. People who are good-hearted, open-minded and well-intentioned have the ability to see the many beauties of life and that humanity is a paradise. Schemers always look on the dark side of things, are anxious about everything, are forever taking precautions, are often in a state of chronic anxiety and in the end live a miserable life. Life exists as you yourself perceive it, be placid in mind and body and the world will also be at peace.

274. The body is like an unmoored boat that may drift or stop at will; the mind is like charred wood, scraping it with the knife of criticism or daubing it with the fragrance of praise is of no account.

Life must be tempered and cultivated, but not in order to complicate it or to make it busier but to make it more natural and smoother and make body and mind rather like an unmoored boat that can float free and unconfined in a calm or in a storm. Thereafter, with a carefree and independent spirit, one may ignore the praise or condemnation of others and express one's ability and exercise one's talents to the full in any situation, thus realizing the perfect "self."

275. It is human nature to take pleasure in the sound of the song of the oriole and to loathe the croaking of frogs, to see flowers and seek to grow them but to see grass and want to cut it. This is to act in terms of form. Were one to observe all in terms of heavenly nature, then what sound is there that is not music and what grass is there that is not life?

Everything in the world has its own function. But in life it is easy for us to judge what is right and what is wrong on the basis of our own prejudices and to decide upon what to take and what to leave upon the basis of our own sense of good and bad. This kind of conduct is influenced by subjective moods and can in no way explain the true nature of the right or wrong or good or bad of matter, either material or immaterial. In considering both things and people one cannot just make judgments upon a subjective view, or upon a momentary whim as to what is good or bad, and keep or discard according to how one feels. Everything in the universe is equal and insofar as the knowledgeable are concerned one should cultivate an equality of mind that does not suffer from material anxiety.

276. When the hair thins and teeth fall out, then is the time to allow our illusory form to wither away; it is in the song of birds and the blooming of flowers that one may know the "suchness" and permanence of one's original mind and true nature.

Birth, age, illness and death are different stages of life that all must experience. If there is birth there must also be death, rise and fall, bloom and wither. Things are born and things die, this is an inevitable natural law. The body is merely a combination of cause and illusion and so we should not be excessively distressed at its deterioration. What is important is to live life according to one's original nature, to meet events with equanimity, to treasure the beauty in the present, to live simply and optimistically and to take pleasure in each day.

277. To be immersed in desire is like a storm in a freezing pond, or to be amongst hills and forests but unable to enjoy tranquility; to be empty of desire or demands is like being cool on a hot night or in a noisy market place but unaware of the hubbub.

The mind of man may be compared to a pool that because of the cravings that occupy it ceaselessly bubbles away; the undistracted mind is as if empty and cannot therefore be contaminated by the noise of the mundane world. The Zen Master Huineng observed two monks arguing, one saying that the flag was moving, the other that the wind was moving hence the flag moved. Huineng said: "You are both wrong, it is your minds that are moving." Having attained *xujing* (a condition in which the spirit enters a state of utter peace where there is no desire, no sense of gain and loss and no achievement or advantage), it is then possible to observe the changes and transformations in things without being disturbed by them.

278. The more you amass the greater your loss, thus it is that riches are not better than the absence of anxiety in poverty; the higher you climb, the harder you fall, thus it is that elevated status is not better than the peace of poverty.

Things taken to an extreme will move in reverse, problems must be investigated dialectically. The more wealth a person amasses, the higher the position he achieves, the greater the danger. The wise person perceives the principle in this and thus does not lose himself in wealth and power. Even if little wealth is attained and one's career is disappointing, one's heart remains as happy as ever. One should consider the joys of humble poverty even if situated in circumstances of great wealth. Treat people well, delight in virtue and take pleasure in charity. Those of exalted rank should consider the suffering of ordinary people and use their position to better the people's lot.

279. Reading the Book of Changes *by the window at dawn and grinding cinnabar ink in the dew from pine needles; chanting sutras at the table at noon while the jade chimes tinkle in the breeze that blows beneath the bamboos.*

This conveys an atmosphere of secluded and carefree rural charm, a picture of the ideal life of the scholar official retiring to live as a hermit. A life of secluded study that transcends the red dust has always been a revered model in Eastern wisdom. It is precisely because this world is so full of noise and clamor that there is such a need for tranquility. An ordered life with poetry and calligraphy as companions, the glimmer of an oil lamp and a statue of the Buddha, all regulated by the sound of the temple bell and drum, contains a peace and calm difficult to achieve in the world of red dust.

280. The flower in a pot in the end tires of life; the bird in a cage loses its charm. Better the brightly patterned flowers and birds of the hills, soaring at will, allowing our spirit to wander the heavens in freedom.

Daoists seek independence and freedom in life and regard the rules of the mundane world as an axe for the felling of nature. King Wei of Chu (?–329 BC) of the period of the Warring States sent an emissary to invite Zhuangzi to leave the hills and become a minister. Zhuangzi asked the emissary: "Would a sacred tortoise be willing to be slaughtered at the hands of men for its shell to become a tool for divination in a temple? Or would it want to live on and crawl around in the mud?" The emissary replied: "Of course it would want to live on and crawl around in the mud." Zhuangzi replied: "In that case, please go back, I would still like to crawl around freely in the mud."

281. It is only because people of the mundane world believe that the word "self" is so significant that there are so many obsessions and vexations. Our forebears said: "If one did not know of the existence of self how would one then know to place value upon external things?" They also said: "Knowing that one's body is not self, how then could one be troubled by vexation?" That is truly a penetrating statement.

People have always regarded themselves as too important and have become attached to the pursuit of selfish desires, happy when they are achieved but upset when they are not. Thus, someone who fully comprehends the secrets of life and the mysteries of the universe will resolutely strike down the attachment to self, realize that the externalities beyond the body are all empty illusions, will no longer suffer an attachment to external things and will no longer suffer vexation. This is the life of enlightenment.

282. Perceive one's youth from age and eliminate haste and struggle; perceive luxury from hardship and eradicate extravagance.

If one experiences the mutability of life and sees its illusory dreamlike nature one will realize that, whatever prominence one achieves, that state cannot be permanent and that it will inevitably encounter a low point, and that with just a little more calm imperturbability one need not always be thinking of wealth and glory. In particular, when self-satisfied, one should concentrate upon the emotion of disappointment and use it to manage one's own longings and desires.

283. It is not always sensible to know the tangled web of men and affairs too thoroughly. Shao Yong said: "In the past they spoke of me, but now they speak of he. I know not to whom the me of today will belong in the future." Were men always to see things like this, it would unknot their tangled hearts.

Heaven and earth have lasted since antiquity but the life of man is only a hundred years. The affairs of the world change: why should man regard the fleeting and illusory changes of profit and loss, rise and fall in the affairs of man as so important and take them so seriously? In the face of the impermanence of the affairs of the world man should preserve his original flawless nature, discard the search for fame and wealth, treat people with sincerity, abandon the bias towards self and deal with life with freedom and ease.

Translator's note: Shao Yong (1012–1077), a well-known scholar of the Neo-Confucian Rationalist School.

284. A cold eye in the midst of excitement will save much trouble; enthusiasm in the midst of desolation will secure true delight.

One should not be carried away by self-satisfaction and should remember that: "The arrogance of wealth and position leaves calamity in its wake." One should remain clearheaded and cool in order to prevent climbing high and then falling heavily. Do not be desolate when disappointed in life; "While the forest grows green, there'll be firewood to burn." As long as you do not lose heart you can keep fighting.

285. If there is a realm of joy then there is a corresponding realm of misery; if there is a fortunate event then it is set off by an unfortunate event. It is only ordinary fare and simple conditions that can be the true home of peace and happiness.

Seen dialectically, all phenomena in the world exist in mutual correspondence. Thus, if joy then suffering, if good then bad. Under certain conditions, the extremes of these corresponding states may be mutually transformed. Consequently, a life of excessive ups and downs, of great joys and tragedies, is not better than maintaining a peaceful space in an ordinary environment. An ordinary life is truly more real and longer lasting.

286. Draw wide the curtains and gaze aloft, see the clouds drawn in and out of the green hills and clear water and know the existence of the great principles of the universe; the bamboos flicker and sway, swallows and doves come and depart at their appointed season, know that identity may merge with matter so that both are forgotten.

The Daoists sought a state of unity between man and heaven and regarded the landscape of hills and water as an embodiment of the ideals of life. The beauty and tranquility of natural scenery creates a longing in the heart. It does no harm to take time from the bustle of the mundane world to return to the hills and water and find consolation and nurture for heart and soul amidst the sound and scent of birds and flowers, to ease the suffering and anxiety of life and thus feel ease of body and soul where both self and the material are forgotten.

287. To know of success is to know that there must be defeat, hence one need not be too resolute in the search for success; to know of life is to know that there is death also, hence one need not be too industrious in the preservation of life.

There is rough and smooth to the path of life and ups and downs in the process of business; nothing is immutable. If there is gain, there must also be loss, if there is success there must also be defeat. Life and death, success and defeat, this kind of growth and decay is a natural law and not subject to the will of man. Once one comprehends this principle one will not reach judgments in affairs on the basis of a temporary success or defeat. The same principle applies to life and to death.

288. A learned monk said: "The bamboo shadow sweeps but the dust on the steps does not move, the moon follows its course but the waters of the pond bear no trace." A scholar of Confucius said: "No matter how fast the water flows my heart remains calm; no matter how much the blossom falls my mind remains at rest." Were man to adopt this attitude in dealing with people and events, how comfortable then would both mind and body be.

There is nowhere that the temptations of the disruptions of the red dust and confusions of lascivious sight and sound do not exist. In the face of these temptations, Confucianists, Buddhists and Daoists all advocate the maintenance of peace of mind. It is only by transcending the temptations of the senses, by not being led astray by anything, by maintaining an attitude of detached calm and natural sincerity, that one is able to lead a life free of restraint.

289. In stillness, to hear the sighing of pines in the forest and the sound of spring water flowing over stones is to know the tinkling of jade on the apparel of the natural world; in leisure, to see the mist at the edge of grass and the shadow of clouds on the pool is to know the greatest achievement of the working of the principles of the universe.

The distinction between the ordinary person of fame and profit and the exceptional man lies in the fact that the former spends his life in the pursuit of wealth and fame and the latter enjoys the leisured and peaceful appreciation of the most beautiful scenery on earth. The beauty of hills and water lies there to behold every day; the question is whether or not you have the temperament and qualities to appreciate it. "Each flower a world and each leaf a Buddha." Discard the vulgar cast of mind of the world of dust and only then will you discover the might and beauty of the creator of the universe.

290. To see for oneself the devastation of the Western Jin, yet still to flaunt the naked blade of power; to know that one's body is destined for the foxes and rabbits of the tombs of Mount Beimang, yet still to amass wealth. The saying has it: "The wild beast may be subjugated but the will of man is difficult to control; the river gulley may be filled, but the heart of man is hard to satisfy." So it is!

The devils from without are easily repelled, it is the devil within the heart that is difficult to eradicate. A man's heart is the most difficult of all to fathom, and also to satisfy. Most errors arise from a single mistaken thought and most evil occurs through the ferment of swelling desire. The life of man is a place of self-cultivation. The crux of self-cultivation is to smash through the illusory world, sweep aside the perplexities of attachment and overcome one's own inner attachments and desires to achieve a stable and peaceful life through a state of mind freed from anxiety.

Translator's note: Mount Beimang at Luoyang in Henan Province is the site of the imperial tombs of the Han dynasty, which preceded the Western Jin (265–316) dynasty by some years.

291. Where neither wind nor wave disturbs the pool of the mind, then all is the blue of hills and the green of water; where one's original nature cherishes all that is good, then fish leap and birds soar.

The interest of life is founded upon the perceptions and feelings of the inner mind and everything external is a projection of self. When the inner mind is darkly clouded, then to look at the hills is to inevitably add layers of anxiety to their appearance; when the inner mind blazes with sunshine then the green waters appear untroubled. Similarly, if the inner mind is filled with hatred, then all is regarded with ferocity; if the inner mind is full of love and joy then the whole world brims with vitality.

292. The official resplendent in cap and sash who one morning sees a peasant at ease in a straw coat and bamboo hat cannot but avoid a sigh of envy; the noble accustomed to extravagant surroundings who one day encounters the calm of plain hangings and uncluttered tables cannot but feel affection for them. Why should man be driven by the ox of wealth or tempted by the stallion of desire rather than seek a life suitable to his inner nature?

The weakness of the character of man lies in the saying "To inhabit good fortune but not to know it," thus the wearer of cap and sash envies the straw coat and bamboo hat; the dweller in luxury fondly recalls the plain hangings and clear tables. In fact, there is a reason for the existence of any lifestyle and it has an interest of its own, the key is whether or not it suits you. As long as it is in keeping with your true nature then it is both the most reasonable and the best. Contrariwise, if it offends your natural temperament and always involves the pursuit of fame and profit, no true happiness will ever come of it.

293. A fish lives because of water but has forgotten the existence of water; a bird flies because of wind but does not know that wind exists. To know this is to transcend the bonds of matter and take joy in the mysteries of heaven.

Man in the mundane world is like a fish swimming in water or a bird flying in the sky; the contented life cannot be separated from various states and conditions. In order to become one with these states and conditions one must be skilled at avoiding attachment to them and being enslaved by the external material world or engulfed by material desire. One should seek the path of spiritual self-cultivation to achieve psychological balance and calm so as to appreciate the true joy of life.

294. Foxes sleep amongst tumbled bricks, rabbits scamper through deserted terraces, these are the scenes of former celebration; the dew on yellow chrysanthemums and the mist amongst the withered grass, these are the battlefields of the past. What is rise and fall? Whence strength and weakness? The very thought is desolation.

The palaces of ministers and princes, the sites of singing and dancing, lie scattered in the twinkling of an eye, leaving just tumbled buildings and empty halls, shriveled grass and withered trees. Faced with the ruins of history everyone must feel regret for the ever-changing world and the impermanence of life, and a sense of dejection and helplessness. Nevertheless, if you realize that this is a natural law not subject to the will of man then it should become easier to bear with equanimity.

295. Take no account of either favor or disgrace, lazily watch the courtyard flowers blossom and fall; do not mind whether you stay in office or become a hermit, gaze in leisure as the clouds in the sky furl and unfurl.

As we live in the world it is difficult to catch a favorable wind. There are few evergreen trees in official life and wealth always reaches the point of exhaustion. In most situations there is more loss than gain and more suffering than joy. In the face of all the circumstances of life, to be able to temper oneself to feel no joy at acquisition, sorrow at loss, fear of favor or disgrace, concern about retention or retirement, to maintain peace of mind and natural simplicity, that is the realm of the superior person and the feeling of the adept.

296. The bright sky and shining moon, where may one not soar, but the flying moth alone makes for the lighted candle; clear springs and fresh fruit, what is there that may not be eaten or drunk, but the owl prefers rotting rats. Oh! Those who are neither moth nor owl, how many truly are you?

We are puzzled when we see a moth fly into the candle flame or an owl eat rotting flesh. It is easy to observe objects, but one's own behavior? There are times when we know quite clearly that we are mistaken, but we persist in continuing in our mistakes, gradually getting into difficulty, caught between "I dare not" and "I cannot give up." The roads of the world are extensive and things to be done more than numerous. There is no need to press forward along a single path. Discard the attachment to the external material world and only then will you be able to advance and withdraw at will.

297. One does not think of disposing of a raft until one is upon it, this is the way of thinking of the unencumbered adept; to seek a donkey while riding one, that is no way to become a Zen master.

The *Diamond Sutra* says that the teachings of Buddha are rather like a raft, it is only there to help you cross a river. Once you have crossed, you dispose of it; you cannot carry it on your back. The truly enlightened person does not become entangled in the intricacies of Buddhist texts. It is only the practitioner whose mind is unencumbered who achieves this kind of enlightened state. The Zen School says that to possess the Buddha nature oneself and yet to seek it outside is as ridiculous as searching for a donkey while riding one. To have Buddha in one's soul yet not to know it is the greatest stupidity of all. The truth is not to be sought externally; it lies within your own soul.

*298. The powerful appear as dragons and heroes seem
like tigers. But considered with a colder eye they look
like ants around an odor and flies competing for blood;
right and wrong are like a swarm of bees and profit
and loss like hedgehog spines. Considered with a colder
nature they are like molten metal or melted snowflakes.*

The man who exhausts his vitality in mutual deception and
the pursuit of wealth and fame is desolate indeed. Life is
short and bitter and years are wasted. If one cannot stand
detached from the world then one will be engulfed by it.
One must view the world with a dispassionate eye and
ought to deal with matters calmly. Glory easily passes,
good things do not last. If one can grasp this principle,
then it will be natural to eliminate the concept of the
pursuit of right and wrong and profit and loss.

299. Be trapped by material desire and feel the misery of your life; linger in the truth of one's character and feel the joy of life. Know the misery and the dust will be dispelled; know the joy and you will reach the sacred realm.

If all that remains of life is materialism and desire and you are left empty-handed with nothing to take away, wandering amidst suffering each day, then that kind of life is pitiful. Wake up to truth, be thankful for kindness and cherish others, live in the moment, behave well and treat all well, then you will be able to rise above the material level, reach the sacred state and experience the richness and perfection of life.

300. When the heart holds not a drop of material desire, then it is as if a furnace flame has consumed a snowflake and the sun has melted ice; when the eye is bright and free, then it is as if the moon hangs in the dark sky and is reflected in the water.

Buddhists believe that every living thing contains the Buddha nature. Each person's heart contains an original nature that shines as bright and carefree as the moon, except that it is covered and corrupted by the worldly desires of greed, anger and stupidity. If we can think less of and see through and nullify profit and loss, favor and disgrace, and be less materialistic, then we can be more well-ordered, see our nature clearly and comprehend the mysteries of heaven. On the other hand, if our desires are too extensive, our selfishness too deep, then the spirit will be deceived to the point where the mind becomes utterly confused and cannot comprehend reason or the principle of things.

301. On Baling Bridge in poetic mood, I finish a whispered recitation beneath the vastness of the mountains and forests; filled with the sense of nature I wander the winding banks of Lake Jing. Walking alone, the hills and rivers reflect each other.

A view of the realm of nature seen aesthetically can stimulate a sense of romantic charm. The cool breezes and bright moon and the romantic charm itself are available to all without the payment of a single coin. Thus, the elegance of poetry does not lie in wealth and prestige but in transcending the world of red dust and escaping from the mundane. Those who trundle on in the red dust through the pools of desire taste the stress and anxieties of life. If, at this point, one can calmly comprehend the tranquility of life and yet still be in a position to perceive the desires harbored in the depths of the soul, then joy may be for ever.

302. Those who stay low will fly high, the early blossom will soon wither. Know this and one may avoid setbacks and curb impatience.

The *Records of the Grand Historian of China* relates that during the Warring States period, King Wei of Qi (378–320 BC) ruled for three years and did nothing. The prime minister, Chunyu Kun (c. 386–c. 310 BC) tactfully enquired: "In your majesty's realm there is a large bird that has lodged in the royal palace for three years. It has neither taken wing nor uttered a sound. May I enquire whether or not your majesty is acquainted with this bird?" The king replied: "This bird may not have flown but when it does it will soar the heavens; it has not made a sound but when it does it will astonish us all." Thereupon he issued a number of decrees and the nation soon became prosperous, strong and well governed. The ancients often said: "Endurance makes steel," this is at the heart of those who achieve much. When keeping a low profile, one must exercise fortitude, build up spirit and strength and wait until the time is ripe, act when necessary and in the end, success will be achieved at a single stroke.

303. It is not until the tree is bare that you regret the passing glory of its foliage; it is not until you are in your coffin that you realize the irrelevance of progeny and wealth.

As life approaches its end, the glory of the past is scattered to the four winds; however much wealth may have been accumulated, it has not the least use. Consequently, the passing of glory and wealth like a wisp of smoke is nothing to worry about. If one meditates and cultivates mind and body throughout life in the realization of principle and the attainment of the Way, acts with virtue every day and accumulates happiness, then, apart from the superficial glory, it may actually be possible to leave something permanent.

304. The true void is not void: an attachment to external image is not truth, nor is destruction of that image the truth—ask the Buddha, "How would you proceed?" In the world, abandon the world: to be swayed by desire is to suffer, to extinguish desire is also to suffer, heed one's self and cultivate virtue.

When Buddhism teaches: "All things are void," the purpose is to prevent us forming an attachment to things that are impermanent. However, to regard everything as void because of this and to believe that the void contains nothing at all would be to fall into a pool of stagnant water where life would be without vitality or interest and not worth living. The void is not utterly empty but should not be the object of attachment. Similarly, unbridled desire is suffering but giving up desire completely is also suffering. The crux is how to sublimate and transform desire. Only by turning one's selfish desires to love for others and for all sentient beings can one reach that supreme portal to the practice of Buddhism.

305. The strong in faith may make a present of 1,000 chariots, the covetous man will quarrel over a copper coin, these are the heights and depths of moral character, for love of fame is no different from love of profit; the son of heaven governs the state, the beggar cries for his supper, as far apart as heaven and earth, but what difference is there between anxiety of mind and anxiety of voice?

Having money brings the anxiety of having it, having no money brings the worry of being without it. People are rich or poor and high or low in status and each different from the other in lifestyle but each has their own joy and their own suffering. Happiness in life does not depend upon social status or official position but upon whether or not there is the ability to transcend. Otherwise, in seeking fame or scheming for profit there is no qualitative difference between emperor or beggar.

306. Well versed in the ways of the world and despite its storms and clouds I am yet disinclined to see it clearly; were I master of human emotion I would merely nod if called an ox or horse.

To be utterly acquainted with all the ways of the mundane world brings neither sorrow nor joy. The deeper one's experience of human nature the less one's interest in the stratagems of the mundane world. In this world there are loyal and devoted friends, there are also treacherous and two-faced rogues. One should treasure the former whilst the latter are not worth a glance. When you are in power others will do everything to seek your favor and speak well of you. When you are on bad terms others will ignore you and gossip maliciously. You should take no account of this and bear no ill will.

307. People today seek detachment but in the end cannot achieve it. One may gradually achieve a state of detachment only by not becoming mired in past thought, not entertaining future thought, and not being attached to present thought.

"Detachment" (*wunian*) is a profound Zen state and has the meaning of the prevention of the growth of distracting thoughts. However, there are many practitioners of Zen who have a one-sided attachment to the concept of no thought at all. In fact, this is impossible. Amongst the confusion of thought and ideas, the maintenance of an imperturbable tranquility of mind is the only way towards the truth and message of detachment. The *Diamond Sutra* says: "The mind of the past is not to be had, the mind of the present is not to be had, and the mind of the future is not to be had." Do not become attached to the thoughts of the past, present or future and the troubled mind may be made stable and vexation become enlightenment.

308. The random thought may become a state of enjoyment and natural objects appear in simple truth; add decoration and their attraction is reduced. Bai Juyi said: "The thought is best in non-action and the wind clearest in nature." Words of wisdom worth pondering.

Even if mankind craftily steals the constructs of heaven it can never match the divine skills of nature. Even if the flower in the pot is beautiful it has lost the charm of nature. Compared with the society of man, nature is simpler and purer, its appeal longer lasting. By investing one's emotions in the landscape of hills and water and forgetting profit and loss for a while, one can then, in a state of oblivion to self and things, experience the most natural interest of life. Looking back at those in the world of bureaucracy who always have an aim in mind and flatter and fawn, one discovers that they are exceptionally ill-visaged. The treasure of all things is in nature and the treasure of life is in its own nature.

309. If one is pure in nature, even were one to eat and drink as it took one's fancy, it would still benefit body and soul; if one is avaricious in character, even were one to discourse upon Zen and recite gatha *verses, it would be mere playing with words.*

In the society of today, the discussion of Zen and Daoism has become a fashion. In no way, however, does this represent genuine practice or actual evidence. No effect can be seen in anything merely by seeking the form and not the essence and not considering the consequences. True practice does not lie merely in fine words but in effort spent on realities. A man of a corrupt and darkened soul may talk Zen all his life but it will be of no help in his spiritual emancipation.

*310. Within the heart of man there is a state of truth,
content in itself without silken strings or bamboo pipes,
fragrant of itself with neither incense nor tea. But
there must be purity of thought and an emptiness of
state, a forgetfulness of vexation and liberation from
the body before one may wander freely within it.*

Buddhism teaches that everyone has the Buddha nature
within them and that all living things may become Buddha;
it is just that the purity of the Buddha nature is often
corrupted by sensual desire, fame, and profit. The Zen
Master Shenxiu said:

> "The body is a bodhi tree
> And the mind a bright mirror and its stand,
> Polished and swept
> Clean of the dust of the world."

If one wants to awaken the bright Buddha nature of the
mind, the mind corrupted by fame and profit must always
be polished clean. However much man is misled by the
scented flowers of the external world, how can they
compete with the fragrance of spiritual enlightenment?
Just empty body and mind and seek within oneself and you
will be able to see the true realm of life and live in life's
true nature.

*311. Gold is mined in the hills and jade grows
from rock, but without illusion their truth cannot
be attained; the Way may be found in wine and
immortals encountered amongst flowers, even elegance
cannot be separated from the commonplace.*

Nobody is born with innate elegance of character; they
may well have grown up in very ordinary circumstances.
The key is the tempering and refining of character
that they may have undergone later. Life is a process of
extracting the fine from the coarse, removing the false but
keeping the true. The true nature of man is very important
and can determine the direction in which someone
develops. Ore must be refined before it can become gold,
jade must be polished and carved before it can be made
into ornaments. Man too must experience storms and
tempests before he can achieve true spiritual maturity.

312. All living things in heaven and earth, every emotion in human relations, each matter in the world, seen with an ordinary eye, each and every one is different; viewed with the eye of the Way, they are all the same. Why draw distinctions? Why choose some but abandon others?

All living things on earth, hills, rivers, grass and trees, the manifold emotions of a family, even extending to the loss and gain, advantage and disadvantage inherent in everything in the world, seen through the eyes of an ordinary man, appears as an unbearable confusion of loose ends. However, if they are seen through the eyes of the enlightened all these very different things appear fundamentally the same in nature. There is no distinction between high and low or noble and base. Consequently, there is no need for any sense of distinction or the adoption of attitudes of love and hate or acceptance or rejection.

313. Sleeping sweetly under a coarse cotton quilt one enjoys the comforts of both heaven and earth; satisfied after a meal of pigweed and plain rice, one knows the truth of the simple life.

Living amidst all sentient beings, it is difficult to avoid becoming entangled by fame and profit. Once enslaved and blinded by greed it is not easy to perceive the beauty of heaven and earth or comprehend the true meaning of life. In the end, having experienced happiness and anger, grief and joy, and tasted all its flavors, one finally discovers that "mild" is the true essence of life. Material wealth may be sufficient to bring happiness for a while but spiritual wealth can bring happiness for life. Consequently, the best way to obtain happiness is to remain optimistic and avoid the influence of external materialism.

314. Entanglement and release lie within the mind, if the mind comprehends, then even the butcher's shambles and the wine shop dregs can become the land of purity (sukhavati). Otherwise, even a liking for the qin and the flight of cranes, flowers and plants, pure though it may be, will always hold the demon of temptation. The saying goes: "With enlightenment one can live in the world of dust as if it were the realm of truth, without it, a monk may as well be a commoner." What truth!

Entanglement and release are determined by the mind. Daoxin (580–651) sought the path of release from the third Zen patriarch Sengcan (c. 510–606) who asked him: "Who was it who entangled you?" Daoxin replied: "There was nobody else." Sengcan said: "Since nobody else entangled you, why do you seek release from somebody else?" At these words, Daoxin was suddenly enlightened.

315. Living carefree in a humble hut, why should I envy gilded beams that reach the clouds or beaded curtains against the rain? Three cups of wine and truth of itself appears, I strum the qin *beneath the crescent moon or play a flute in the breeze.*

An abundant materialism requires objective conditions but spiritual joy may be built anywhere at any time. Happiness in life does not depend upon whether your house is spacious or not, or upon the delicacy of your cuisine, but upon whether you are openhearted or not and whether you are happy by nature.

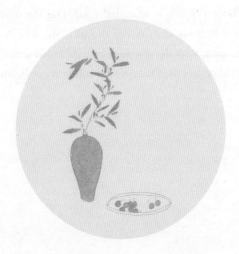

316. In the solitude of the sounds of nature, I suddenly hear the chirping of a bird that calls up a sense of remote tranquility; when the autumn undergrowth is cleared, I suddenly see a single stem that flourishes still and arouses feelings of limitless vitality. Thus, it can be seen that one's innate nature does not always wither and that vitality is easily sparked.

In the course of life there are always episodes of weariness and despair, rather like wandering through a barren autumn landscape. When one wearies of the road ahead, it does no harm to remind oneself that vitality is stored throughout the world, so there is no need to be dispirited or to blame or pity oneself. Far from it, one should summon up one's spirits and mobilize the will to fight on.

317. The poet Bai Juyi said: "Better to free mind and body and blindly let nature take its course." Another poet, Chao Buzhi, said: "Better to curb mind and body and return to a state of calm restraint." Those that let free will deteriorate into ferocity and those that exercise restraint will enter a state of barren desolation. Those that manage mind and body with skill and maintain their grip may curb or let go at will.

Unrestrained freedom will always degenerate into unbridled license; those that stick inflexibly to rules and convention will lose the natural interest of life. Only by combining the two attitudes can one curb or let free one's senses at will and do as one wishes.

Translator's note: Chao Buzhi(1053–1110), a well-known writer of the Northern Song dynasty.

*318. On a snowy night when the moon brightens the
heavens, so is the mind limpid and clear; come the
balmy winds of spring, the senses brim with ease. Mind
and nature are seamlessly combined.*

Traditionally, there has always been the concept of "Heaven
and man as one" in Chinese culture. Man's mind and nature
are an inseparable single common entity. The inexhaustible
spirit of the poet is aroused by cool breezes and the bright
moon and by the beauty of fine mornings, though the
misery of grey clouds and driving rain will add to his
limitless sorrow. The scenery of nature is an expression of
the mind of man. Man expresses his aspirations through
the changes in nature, he also refines his own nature
through them.

319. Writing proceeds through simplicity and the Way is attained through simplicity, even a simple word has boundless significance. As Tao Yuanming wrote in his Record *of the* Peach Garden, *"Dogs bark in the peach orchard and cocks crow amongst the mulberries," such simplicity is this. As for the moon mirrored in a cold pool or the crow in the bare tree, one feels that in the midst of all this delicate skill there lies a melancholy.*

The traditional spirit of Confucianism, Buddhism and Daoism valued simplicity and approved a life that was plain, sincere, and natural. It termed sincere, diligent conduct that reduced selfishness and diminished desire as "keeping to simplicity." This spirit was also opposed to a life of extravagance, opportunism and artificiality.

320. Those who are masters of the material world may take no joy in gain but also suffer no sorrow at loss, and wander the world in freedom; those who have been mastered by the material world may suffer resentment in unfavorable circumstances but can also fall prey to greed in favorable circumstances. The slightest thing can cause one to be entangled.

Xunzi said: "The gentleman is master of the material world, the rogue is mastered by the material world." Spirit and mind are the masters of life. Once enlightened, one can use the mind to master the material world and transcend the joy or anxiety of profit and loss; when confused and led by circumstance, the slightest thing may drag one into a mental quagmire. When one's spirit has transcended the external environment and is no longer entangled by outside circumstances, a wider world will appear before one.

321. If the universal principle is still then matter is still also; to abandon matter for principle is as ridiculous as discarding the shadow but keeping the body. If the spirit is void then the external state is void too; discarding the external state and keeping the spirit is like gathering a stink to discourage mosquitos.

The truth of the noumenal world and the phenomena of the apparent world coexist. If the noumenal truth does not exist, then neither do the phenomena of the apparent world. Thinking of leaving the phenomena of the apparent world makes it impossible to gain the noumenal truth. The mind of the unenlightened ordinary person is always obstructed by the external state, however, the enlightened person is able to use the mind to transform the external environment. In the clamor of the ordinary world, the ability to attain a void of mind is a profound accomplishment of inexhaustible benefit.

322. The comforting things of life are always a matter of suiting oneself, hence the pleasure of taking wine without compulsion, the victory of not winning at chess, the joy of playing the tuneless flute, the loftiness of playing an unstrung qin, *the sincerity of unarranged encounters, and the honesty of neither greeting nor seeing off guests. A single hint of the compulsion of convention and one falls into the sea of suffering of the mundane world!*

The most important principle in suiting oneself is not to be bound by form; if one is not bound by everyday convention everything will be open and above board. The man of wisdom who is pure in mind may coolly please himself in only seeking things that suit his own original nature in order to achieve spiritual independence. To be able to achieve this is to reach the highest state of life.

323. Imagine one's form and appearance before birth, what was it like? Imagine too the scene after death, what is that like? Then all notion turns to cold ashes and one's nature is stilled, now you may transcend the external material world and wander in the state that existed before form.

The body did not exist before birth; the body still does not exist after death. Once this principle is clear, one realizes that the attachment to the physical body and obsession with the physical world can be eliminated at once. As we live in the world, the most important thing of all is to eliminate obsessions and gain enlightenment.

324. In illness to think of the value of recovery, in chaos to think of the rewards of peace, this is not wisdom or foresight; to be fortunate but to know that it is the root of disaster, to be greedy for life but to know that it is the cause of death, that is wisdom!

One should always be crystal clear about the fulcrum of events. However, in real life people have to experience setbacks and suffering before they are able to achieve any deep understanding of the principles involved. One has to lose freedom to know its value and to be ill to know the importance of health. It is better to take precautions in advance than to know and be aware later. Once you have seen through to the principle of life and death and grasped the causes of success and failure, then you can live a life of unencumbered self-assurance.

325. The actor powders and paints, showing both beauty and ugliness at the tip of a brush. Soon the singers are scattered and the dancers disperse; where is the beauty and ugliness then? The chess players battle back and forth, win or lose piece by piece. Soon the game is over and the pieces housed; where is the victory and defeat then?

In the endlessness of time and the vastness of heaven and earth, the greatest achievement of riches and honor is like a passing cloud that leaves not a trace. Once one has realized this truth, what is the point of brooding over success and failure, gain and loss entangled in suffering? Why bother to waste time in unscrupulous scheming after wealth and position?

*326. Only those with peace of mind may be master of
the natural elegance of flowers in the wind or the clear
brightness of the moon in snow; only the leisured may
know the truth of the glory and wither of the water and
trees or the growth and decay of bamboo and rocks.*

For those exhausted by rushing about amidst the affairs
of the mundane world, true carefree leisure is difficult
to attain. The mind is entangled in profit and fame, the
eye sees nothing but success and failure and gain and
loss, and the problems of self and other, right and wrong,
continuously afflict the spirit. Clear the vulgar eye of
smoke and dust and exchange it for the eye of wisdom and
one will realize that what one sees is very different. Wind
and flowers, snow and moon, the landscape of grass and
trees are all phenomena without innate emotion. Approach
them with an attitude of peace and tranquility, however,
and one may experience their inner delight.

327. Talk to the farmer in his fields of glazed chicken and sorghum spirit and he will be delighted, ask him about fine food and elegant delicacies and he will know nothing; speak of brown gowns and coarse cloth and he will naturally be happy, enquire of splendid robes and imperial costume and he will have no acquaintance. His world is complete and hence his demands are moderate, this is the highest state of life.

The spirit of those in the red dust is distraught but their desires boil. The nature of those who live in the countryside is entire and their expectations are modest. The happiness of the country dweller lies in a pure simplicity, they have no desires beyond plain tea and simple food. This kind of life may be harsh but it is a long way from the exhaustion and anxiety of the world of red dust. Gentle breezes blow and rice blossom emits its fragrance; it may well be considered an earthly paradise.

328. There is no mind to the mind, why then the need to examine it? The Buddhists say that to examine the mind increases its obstacles; all matter was originally one, why then seek to make it whole? Zhuangzi said that making it whole was instead to sunder the unity of all things.

The Zen Master Huineng said:

> "The beginning had no substance,
> Where then was the dust?"

The nature of man was originally pure and limpid, where did the dust come from? If one always emphasizes the sweeping away of dust and the cultivation of body and mind it is rather like adding waves to the pool of a mind that is already windless and calm. The large and small, long and short, beautiful and ugly, high and low of everything in the world are all different in state, but seen through the eyes of heaven there is fundamentally absolutely no distinction at all; they were originally an integral whole. If we can dissect the commonalities from the whole, why cannot the idea of their distinctions have already existed in the mind?

329. When the music and song is at its peak and to be able to sweep off without a qualm, how one should admire the enlightened who can let go at the last minute; when the water-clock has dripped dry at dead of night but still to continue restlessly rushing about, how laughable are the commonplace people thus immersed in a sea of suffering.

Never take things to the point of losing interest or strive to reach the extreme, but stop when it seems just right; that is the ideal. It is not that life may not be enjoyed; the crux is the ability to maintain a sense of proportion. "Look at the half-opened flower, drink 'til only half drunk." If you have a sense of what is appropriate to the situation, then life may be enjoyed. Similarly, it is not that desires may not be pursued but that one may be led on by desire and consequently suffer its bitterness. If one can understand how to let go and not become excessively attached, then that is a state of unencumbered peace where carefree joy lies before one.

330. When one has not yet mastered self-control it is best to distance oneself from the clamor of the mundane world, render the mind unseeing and then meet desire without trouble, so that one may maintain peace of mind; when self-control is mastered then one may mix with the mundane world, allow the mind to see and yet not be troubled, thereby nurturing one's self-developed sense of enlightenment.

From the point of view of the relationship between the external state and the mind, there are three stages to the practice of Buddhism; the first is to borrow from circumstance to adjust the mind, the second is to have no mind for circumstance, and the third is to transform circumstance with the mind. When self-control is as yet unmastered, one should keep one's distance from any external state that engenders desire and nurture spiritual tranquility in a remote and peaceful environment. Once self-control has been empowered, one may enter the red dust of the mundane world without fear of being moved by desire. When this skill has been well developed, the strength of the inner mind can dissolve all temptation and transform the external state. It is this that is the truly great accomplishment.

331. Those who take joy in solitude and hate noise avoid people in order to seek tranquility, not knowing that a desire for the absence of others becomes an attachment to self; the mind attached to tranquility is the root of turmoil. How does one attain a state of regarding both self and other as the same, the realm where movement and stillness are both forgotten?

When the day comes and somebody acquires a sense of distinctions it can give rise to a great deal of anxiety. Those who like solitude and dislike noise hope to gain tranquility by living in the hills and forests as a hermit. It is little understood that this kind of—love this hate that—sense of distinction will, unless eliminated, prevent even the most secluded of hills and forests from bringing any inner peace. This is because the source of restlessness and agitation lies not in the external state of the hills and forests but in the inner mind. To seek only the tranquility of the external state is to abandon the root in favor of the branch, to treat the symptoms rather than the cause.

332. Living carefree in the hills, each and every sight inspires thoughts of beauty: a single cloud or a flock of cranes and thoughts of transcendence arise; the mountain springs and valley streams bring dreams of washing as clean as snow; caress the trunks of juniper and plum and one can follow their indomitable spirit; with elk and egret for company the cunning of the mind is instantly forgotten. Once one enters the world of dust, then even if the material world is out of touch, this body of yours is superfluous.

Confronted by all the beauty of nature it is easy to put fame and profit out of mind. The pace of modern life is fast and with the rapid development of urbanization, the distance between man and nature has become greater and greater, and the joy of the landscape of hills and water is now a luxury. Nevertheless, however busy we may be we should all take the time to get close to nature and experience a different kind of pleasure in life amidst a natural landscape.

333. When the mood takes one, stroll staff in hand amidst a fragrant meadow and the birds of the wild, knowing that one harbors no ill will, can be one's companions; when one achieves a superior understanding of the scenery, falling flowers will drape one's shoulders as one meditates, and the white clouds will linger without a word.

It is possible, in life, to experience fully the noise and bustle of the red dust but it is also possible to fully enjoy the beauty of the tranquility of the natural landscape. One can say of people in the mundane world, who are weary of the red dust, that in a hurried life the act of leaving precious time to appreciate the hills and fields of the natural landscape is a further demonstration of life's multi-dimensional richness. When the spirit is relaxed, to linger intoxicated by the natural scenery is an event of incomparable beauty. Nature and the natural world are a mutually amalgamated seamless combination of the internal and external aspects of life into a universal life.

334. Fortune and misfortune in life are the products of subjective thought. Thus it is that Buddhists say: "The fierce flames of profit and desire are a furnace; immersion in greed and love is a sea of suffering, a single pure thought and the flames turn to water, a single thought of sudden enlightenment and the boat has arrived at the opposite shore." The slightest shift of thought and the state suddenly changes. Beware!

Fortune is born of the mind and misfortune is a creation of the mind. The fortune and misfortune of life are constructs of one's own conceptions. When desire expands and one loses self-control it will always end in tragedy. Throughout the course of life one should always maintain a clear mind. The root of self-cultivation lies in cultivation of the mind, thus one should devote considerable effort to the act of thinking. One can only be in command of oneself by extinguishing the flames of desire and growing a clear-sighted wisdom.

335. Rope may fell a tree and dripping water wear through rock, thus those who study the Way should strive harder; water runs in channels and melons fall when ripe, thus those who have achieved the Way may leave all to the workings of heaven.

Xunzi said: "Without a multitude of steps you cannot travel a thousand *li*, without numbers of small streams there can be no rivers." The establishment of any enterprise requires perseverance, diligence and effort. With these, success is assured. Quantitative change brings qualitative change, unremitting perseverance and the expenditure of effort will always achieve results. It is the half-hearted approach that is to be feared, in the end it gets nowhere and nothing is achieved.

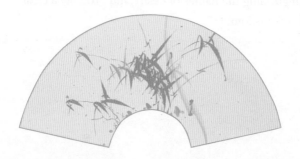

336. When the mind ceases its cunning the moon shines and the breezes blow, and the world is no longer a sea of suffering; for the lofty mind there is no noise of carts or horses' hooves, why need to thirst after hills and woods?

Once the selfish, scheming mind is stilled, life is immediately clear and peaceful, the world of the red dust is no longer a limitless sea of suffering, and the misery of the *saha* world of endurance becomes a paradise. The poet Tao Yuanming wrote in his poem *Drinking Wine*:

> "I've built my hut amidst this world of man,
> Yet without the clatter of horse and cart.
> If you asked how could that be?
> I'd say I float distant from this dusty world …"

As long as the mind is secluded and remote there can be no loss of contentment or tranquility.

337. Trees and grass shed their seed and seedlings
sprout below; bitter cold returns to balmy sun. In
desolate winter a sense of budding life takes first place;
from this we can see the purposes of heaven and earth.

It is often said, "If there is life there must be death, if there is death there must be life." Life and death are a cycle and replace one another, everything in heaven and earth is in a state of continuous re-birth. The life force is already within all sentient beings as yet unborn. An understanding of the laws that govern this cycle is enough to comprehend the rules of conduct. If somebody wishes to acquire skill in the study and analysis of the changes in all the matter and phenomena of the world, to be able to grasp and hold the opportunities of change, they should not be mesmerized by external appearances or withdraw because of a temporary setback, in particular they should not reach conclusions on the basis of momentary success or failure.

338. View the hills after rain and the scene appears in fresh beauty; listen to a temple bell on a still night and the sound is clearer still.

Distant hills seen after rain seem fresh and beautiful with an extra appearance of freshness and beauty. In the stillness of the depth of night, the clamor of the red dust gradually subsides and the sound of a temple bell reaches the ear, clearer and clearer and more and more melodious. This is a world cleansed of dirt and dust, a world shorn of the bustle of activity. The uttermost of everything is clear, bright, secluded and tranquil. Nature provides a perception of beauty through sight and sound and could one taste the qualities of the natural landscape, this would be the best. Viewing the hills after rain and listening to a temple bell in the still of night is enough to dispel the vexations of the scholar and satisfy the tastes of the hermit.

339. Climbing a mountain expands the mental horizons; a view of flowing water elevates the senses. Studying through a night of snow and sleet lightens the spirit; singing loudly on a hilltop emboldens one.

The pleasures and perceptions of life are of different kinds and are expressed differently according to differences of character and temperament. Feelings are purified amongst green hills and clear water, and the mind expands. Climbing high and gazing into the distance arouses a sense of vastness. Viewing flowing water stimulates a feeling of continuity. Perceiving the principle within the landscape of hills and water and following the example of the virtue it contains will imperceptibly nurture both wisdom and integrity. Studying through a night of snow and sleet will lighten body and soul. Shouting to the sky from the top of a hill proclaims boldness to the heavens. Heaven and man as one, their joint spirits aroused.

340. When the mind expands then ten thousand in cash is a mere earthenware pot; a narrow mind is like the wheels of a cart in a rut.

Everything that you see is a reflection of your inner mind. As the mind expands so does the world shrink; to the small-minded all things are large. Emotions determine the pattern of events and this pattern determines the future. The Qin dynasty Prime Minister Li Si said: "Rivers and lakes do not choose to ignore narrow streams, hence their great size." The forward momentum of life cannot escape the surge towards the sea. People often say: "As large as the mind may be, just so large is the stage." The road to success not only requires lofty aspirations, even more does it require broad vision in conduct and the handling of affairs.

341. There can be no nature without wind, moon, flowers and willows; there can be no mind without desire or liking. Self should master matter not matter enslave self, then liking and desire may become the purposes of heaven and the emotions of the world of dust become a state of truth.

Between heaven and earth there is the chattering of birds and the scent of flowers, within the mind there are the Six Emotions and the Seven Desires. The possession of desire is not to be feared, it is to be driven by desire and becoming its slave that is to be feared. In *Zhuangzi* it is said: "Where liking and desire run deep, spiritual nature is shallow." Somebody who lets himself be driven by desire in the unscrupulous acquisition of profit and position will find it extremely difficult to maintain a pure and virtuous disposition. Consequently, a person should continuously undertake self-cultivation and use his own willpower to control material greed, maintain the integrity of his innermost being, and avoid losing direction in life.

342. When self knows self, only then can all sentient beings express their natural being; when that which is heaven's is returned to heaven, only then can one live in this world as if not of it.

When one can see self from the point of view of other than self and abandon the emotions and desires of the dust of the mundane world, then there is no sentient being that is not you, thus you can no longer appropriate all sentient beings to your own use. They all assume their natural place. If there is a desire to possess them for oneself, the result will be a lifetime of unsatisfied craving. Similarly, those who return what is heaven's to heaven will have an unencumbered mind free of desire and, although they may be situated in the dust of the mundane world, they will live easy in the mind. Thus, we should escape the confines of self to ponder problems and throw off the bonds of fame and wealth in order to attain spiritual freedom and ease.

343. Man lives in a world where too much leisure means distracting thoughts spread unchecked and too much activity prevents his true character from appearing. Thus, the gentleman cannot but harbor some anxiety for mind and body but must also have some regard for the pleasures of singing to the wind and playing with the moon.

In life there must be a balance between tension and relaxation and between work and leisure. Pushing oneself too hard and rushing about all day runs the risk of losing interest in life, becoming wearily apathetic, and even of an early death in one's prime. Nevertheless, being excessively relaxed and indulging in ease makes it easy for distracting thoughts to spread and sap the will, resulting in a wasted life.

344. Truth is usually lost from the mind of man through agitation of thought. If there is no thought, then one may sit in calm meditation amidst the cold clarity of falling raindrops as the clouds form and drift away. The call of birds and the falling flowers gladden the heart. Where is the realm that has no truth? What form lacks its own mystery?

Industriously making a living and busily seeking profit, it is difficult to maintain tranquility of spirit. As the mind moves so is material desire born, with the birth of material desire so does suffering arrive. Because of this an aesthetic of calm observation became the universal pursuit of Chinese culture. Objects and occasions that please the emotions and feed the senses are everywhere, the crux is whether or not it is possible to discover and appreciate them. When there is not a single distracting thought it is possible to enjoy the limitless beauty of life and all the living things of nature, the landscapes of the four seasons all become the scenery of the aesthetic. Watch the white clouds and as they drift away so does the mind, listen to the sound of a shower of rain and as it cools so does the heart.

345. As the child is born so is the mother in danger, as cash mounts up so do thieves pry and prey, what joy is there that is without anxiety? In poverty one may economize, in sickness one may protect the body, what anxiety is there that is without joy? Thus it is that the enlightened man, when confronted with the favorable or the unfavorable, dismisses the emotions of both sorrow and joy.

There are two characteristics to everything, advantage and disadvantage follow each other, and good fortune and disaster support each other. If you are unable to deal with these characteristics dialectically and are happy when things go well but miserable when they do not, the time spent in the sadness of the unattainable will far exceed the time spent in joy. The life of man rises and falls, floats and sinks in impermanence, there are times of nobility and times of baseness, of riches and of poverty, times favorable and unfavorable, and times of sunshine and of rain. No matter in what kind of situation you may find yourself, optimism and far-sightedness will enable you to remain calm and collected and to operate with skill.

*346. The ear hears the sound of the wind in a
mountain valley, once it has passed nothing remains
and right and wrong disappear; the mind sees the
moon reflected in a pool, its brightness leaves no trace
and self and matter are forgotten.*

The world of phenomena that man is aware of through
the six sensory organs of eyes, ears, nose, tongue, body
and sense is ever-changing and impermanent. Thus, the
ordinary inhabitants of the mundane world take nothing
for something and regard falsehood as truth, thereby
producing a fierce sense of attachment. Consequently,
the *Diamond Sutra* says: "Do not dwell but let the mind
grow" (no matter where you are, the mind must be free of
attachment and live and grow naturally), and emphasizes
that in caring for all things and phenomena one should
neither be shackled nor corrupted by them. Man should
have no attachment to the substance of the mundane
world, only then will he find his own true mind.

347. The people of the mundane world entangled by honor and advantage are apt to talk of the "world of dust" and "sea of bitterness," unaware of white clouds and blue hills, or flowing rivers and standing stones, welcoming flowers or chirping birds, fishermen's chanting or woodcutters' songs. The world is not dust, nor the sea bitter; the dust and bitterness are the creation of their own minds.

In the beginning there was neither "dust" nor "bitterness" in this world of ours. It is we, unable to escape the bonds of a mindset of fame and profit, who must reap what we have sown, who have obscured ourselves in a state of dust and immersed ourselves in a sea of bitterness. If we could only throw off fame and profit and rid ourselves of the commonplace and vulgar, a pure land would exist between heaven and earth.

348. View the half-opened flower, drink until slightly drunk; there is delight in this. View the flower in full blossom, drink until dead drunk; that is to be in an evil situation. The complacent should consider this.

The moon waxes and wanes, flowers open then wither, the principle of the cycle of waxing and waning has driven the evolution and development of the world since time immemorial. Thus, in Chinese culture: "The Way of heaven abhors excess, the ways of man fear sufficiency." Things should never be overdone and space for maneuver should always be left. So flowers should be admired when semi-opened and drink taken in a state of semi-intoxication. The Confucian doctrine of the mean has been the supreme determinant in the philosophy of conduct in China for the last thousand years.

349. The dishes of the hills are not watered by the world and feathered fowl are not raised by it but their taste is sweet and cool. Were we to avoid the corruption of the ways of the world would not our nature and presence be vastly different?

Daoists believe that the most superior state of conduct lies in the natural and involuntary. If someone is uncorrupted by fame and profit, his moral character and temperament will be exceptionally pure. How then should one preserve one's heaven-given nature? Laozi recommended being aware of the advantages of slippery dealings but nevertheless preferring honesty; being aware of the advantages of flattery but preferring plain speaking; knowing the grandeur of wealth and position but preferring a simple life; knowing the pleasure of eating fine food and delicacies but enthusiastically eating coarse rice and weak tea. This is a pure, natural, original character uncorrupted by the vulgar habits of the mundane world.

350. There is contentment to be found in planting flowers and growing bamboo, in playing with cranes and looking at fish. A mere fondness for scenery and dabbling in nature is like skin-deep Confucianism or the so-called void of the Buddhists; what interest is there to that?

Confucian thought promotes a positive engagement with the world. Even the planting of flowers and bamboo or playing with birds and looking at fish has a value in the ability it bestows to comprehend the interest that lies within it, as well as in character cultivation and self-cultivation so as to serve society better. It is of no real benefit just to be engrossed in the external and lost in its detail to the point that it saps the will, or merely to be a skin-deep Confucianist with a superficial rather than genuine knowledge, as criticized by Confucians. Nor will there be any proper result from being immersed in the state of a nothingness without consciousness or feeling or thought or existence that is so criticized by Buddhists.

351. The scholar in the hills may live in honest poverty but he is rich in inner ease; the peasant in the fields may be low in status but he has a simple good nature. If lost to the corruption of the city, it would be better to die in a ditch with body and soul still pure.

Chinese culture has always placed weight upon righteousness rather than advantage, believing that life may be impoverished but conduct should be upright. The material life of hermit and peasant is very basic, but it is guaranteed by a simplicity of nature. The lofty idealists of Chinese history are all the same, in times of national disaster they would rather die heroically than surrender for the sake of a paltry life. For example, the Southern Song dynasty (1127–1279) prime minister, Wen Tianxiang (1236–1283) died rather than bend the knee to his Yuan (1279–1368) captors, saying in a poem:

"Who is there
Who has never ever died?
I leave a loyal heart
To light the pages of history."

In this he truly practiced the Confucian ideal of "Sacrifice the body to achieve humanity, give up life to gain righteousness."

352. Dubious luck and unexplained gains, if not the bait of the creator, are a trap laid by the mundane world. In this respect, those who lack lofty aspirations rarely escape their wiles.

Heaven does not distribute meat pies, they are just traps deliberately devised by others. One's conduct in the world must be principled, indulge the fantasy of something for nothing and one will take the wrong road. Seeking "dubious luck" is the root of disaster. When others plot, they first seek to satisfy your material desires and unless you are alert you will take the bait, be hooked like a fish or bird, and lose your life. One should not seek more than one's share nor hanker after ill-gotten gains. One should reap no more than one sows. If one thinks to gain, one must first learn to give.

353. Life is like being a puppet on a stage, but with the strings in your hand and untangled, moving freely up and down, starting and stopping at will without interference from others, then you can transcend this stage.

Living in the world, each one of us is like a puppet on a stage. If you wish to control your own fate, then do not allow yourself to be manipulated and entangled by other people and external states. One meets all kinds of temptations in life, they may cause us to lose our original nature and forget our purpose in life. Consequently, we should be skilled in detecting one's strengths and advantages, clearly see one's own innate nature, stand firm, and refuse to be dazzled by beauty or confused by desire. If we can, then we will be able to overcome the manipulation of others and achieve freedom in life.

354. An event occurs and there is harm to life, thus it is that under heaven the absence of events is often regarded as good fortune. I read an ancient poem that said: "Speak not of the vassal kings, a single general's victory is ten thousand broken bones." Also: "Were heaven to command peace on earth, the sheathed sword would not be drawn or begrudge its thousand-year death." Words that, although full of fierce heroism, turn invisibly to hailstones.

Within all the events and matters of mankind there exists a reciprocal cycle of advantage and disadvantage, gain and loss. Things have their benefits but also their blacker side: this is called "fortune is the crumbling of disaster," disaster often lurks within good fortune. As we live in the world our lives continue, we work away, unaware that great blessings are easy to enjoy but the blessings of solitary leisure are difficult to attain: these are the blessings of the absence of events and affairs, only those enlightened in the Way are able to enjoy them.

355. The wanton woman may perversely become a nun, the man greedy for fame may give way to his feelings and follow the Way. Similarly, the gate to the place of purity is often a haunt of depravity.

There are many things in the world that are apparent contradictions but are in fact inevitable. The portal to Buddhism was originally a place of practice for purity but there have always been despicable people who have found their way in. To live in pure contemplation as a hermit in the hills was originally the calling of elegant scholars but it became the road to fame for those who sought it; the affairs of man are strewn in confusion, truth and lies, genuine and false, all piled upon each other; heaven and earth are vast and awash with contradictions.

356. The billowing waves reach the heavens and those in the boat know not fear, but those without are frozen in terror; the drunkard seated cursing at table is not startled but renders bystanders speechless. Thus, the gentleman, though he may be involved in a matter, must seek to be beyond it.

Somebody who is deeply involved in something usually has no sense of fear or danger but is swayed by emotion. When he comes to look at it in the cold light of day he begins to regret, the great mistake has already taken shape and the bitter consequences are hard to swallow. Consequently, when in the midst of events one should adopt an outside stance and point of view that will enable one to gain a clearheaded knowledge of the problem, and with rational consideration and cool handling it will be possible to avoid a regrettable or dreadful outcome.

357. In life, a measure of reduction will bring a measure of detachment: reduce social relationships and disturbance will diminish, talk less and less offence will be given, ponder less and the spirit will be wearied less, be less clever and original innocence will prevail. Those who do not seek to reduce but to add will spend this life in chains!

One may employ addition in an occupation but should be able to use subtraction in self-cultivation. In our society today, shot through with material desire, the process of self-cultivation should include learning the art of *danshari,* the ability to cut off the unwanted, discard the excess and part from one's attachment to things. We should learn to subtract in order to reduce excessive material desires and burdens. We should reduce our social relationships since one close friend is enough; we should talk less because disaster emerges from the mouth; we should ponder less because pondering wearies the spirit; we should be less clever since clever people frequently scheme against others and easily shorten their own lives. Life is very simple, why not live it simply?

358. The summer heat and winter cold of nature are easy to escape, the flames and frigidity of the world of man are difficult to remove; even were the flames and frigidity easy to remove, then the contradictions in our hearts would be difficult to reduce. If these contradictions could be removed, the heart would be filled with joy and the spring breeze would blow everywhere.

Joy and suffering in life are not subjective but objective, in no way do they depend upon whether the weather is hot or cold, or upon the warmth or coolness of social behavior. They are entirely a sensory perception existing amongst the ideas of our inner mind. If it were possible to act on the basis of "Dismiss both person and self, benevolence and grievance are both a void" then neither the hot and cold of mankind nor the hypocrisy of the world would be worth consideration. Consequently, if one treats people on the basis of returning good for evil, it will naturally dissolve previous ill will and fill the heart with joy, so that it is as if a cleansing spring breeze blows at all times and in all places. In this way there need be no arguments about individual right and wrong, or the possibility of being trapped in the distress of personal relationships.

359. Seek not the finest tea and the pot will never run dry; drink not the strongest wine and the cup will never be empty. Play a stringless qin *for melody and blow a tuneless flute for satisfaction. Though you may not aspire to the realm of the emperor Fuxi of legend, you may join the company of the eccentrics Ji Kang and Ruan Ji.*

The people of China enjoyed drinking wine and tea and playing the *qin* and flute but their importance lies not in their outer attributes but upon their inner delight. A bowl of coarse tea may invigorate the palate, a jug of muddy wine may wet the throat, the melody of the stringless *qin* may resemble the music of heaven, and a tuneless flute may be played by instinct alone. The joy and happiness of life has actually always been obtainable through such simple means. The importance lies in the artistic environment, the grace and delight, the transcendence of bearing, the utensils and ceremony, it is this that is the sublime aesthetic state.

Translator's note: Fuxi was the legendary founder of Chinese civilization. Ji Kang (223–262 or 224–263) and Ruan Ji (210–263) were famously eccentric literary and cultural figures of the state of Wei in times of political turmoil during the period of the Three Kingdoms.

360. Buddhists follow cause and affinity and Confucians are content with their place: these two phrases are a raft on which to cross the sea. Thus it is that the roads through life are vast and without end and once you seek the whole, every thread is tangled. Only encounter cause with calm, contentment can only come of engagement.

The Buddhist teaches the concept of "following affinity" and no matter whether good or bad, favorable or unfavorable, losing or gaining, suffering defeat or achieving victory, to follow predestined cause and affinity naturally and without regard to personal gain or loss in simple acceptance. Confucianism teaches contentment with one's position, the ability to perform whatever task in whatever position you hold and according to your role, and not to vainly hanker after things beyond its bounds. People who adhere to these two concepts may pass their life in peace and calm.

To seek perfection in everything is to fall prey to exhaustion and distress. Of course, these two concepts emphasize the need not to be dragged away by desire. Striving to create a peaceful inner mind of rock-like stability does not mean that people should abandon their struggles or aspirations.

Dates of the Chinese Dynasties

Xia Dynasty	2070–1600 BC
Shang Dynasty	1600–1046 BC
Zhou Dynasty	1046–256 BC
Western Zhou Dynasty	1046–771 BC
Eastern Zhou Dynasty	770–256 BC
Spring and Autumn Period	770–476 BC
Warring States Period	475–221 BC
Qin Dynasty	221–206 BC
Han Dynasty	206 BC–AD 220
Western Han Dynasty	206 BC–AD 25
Eastern Han Dynasty	25–220
Three Kingdoms	220–280
Wei	220–265
Shu Han	221–263
Wu	222–80
Jin Dynasty	265–420
Western Jin Dynasty	265–316
Eastern Jin Dynasty	317–420
Northern and Southern Dynasties	420–589
Southern Dynasties	420–589
Liang Dynasty	502–557
Northern Dynasties	439–581
Sui Dynasty	581–618
Tang Dynasty	618–907
Five Dynasties and Ten Kingdoms	907–960
Five Dynasties	907–960
Ten Kingdoms	902–979
Song Dynasty	960–1279
Northern Song Dynasty	960–1127
Southern Song Dynasty	1127–1279
Liao Dynasty	916–1125
Jin Dynasty	1115–1234
Xixia Dynasty (or Tangut)	1038–1227
Yuan Dynasty	1279–1368
Ming Dynasty	1368–1644
Qing Dynasty	1644–1911